ELLEN TERRY
The Painter's Actress

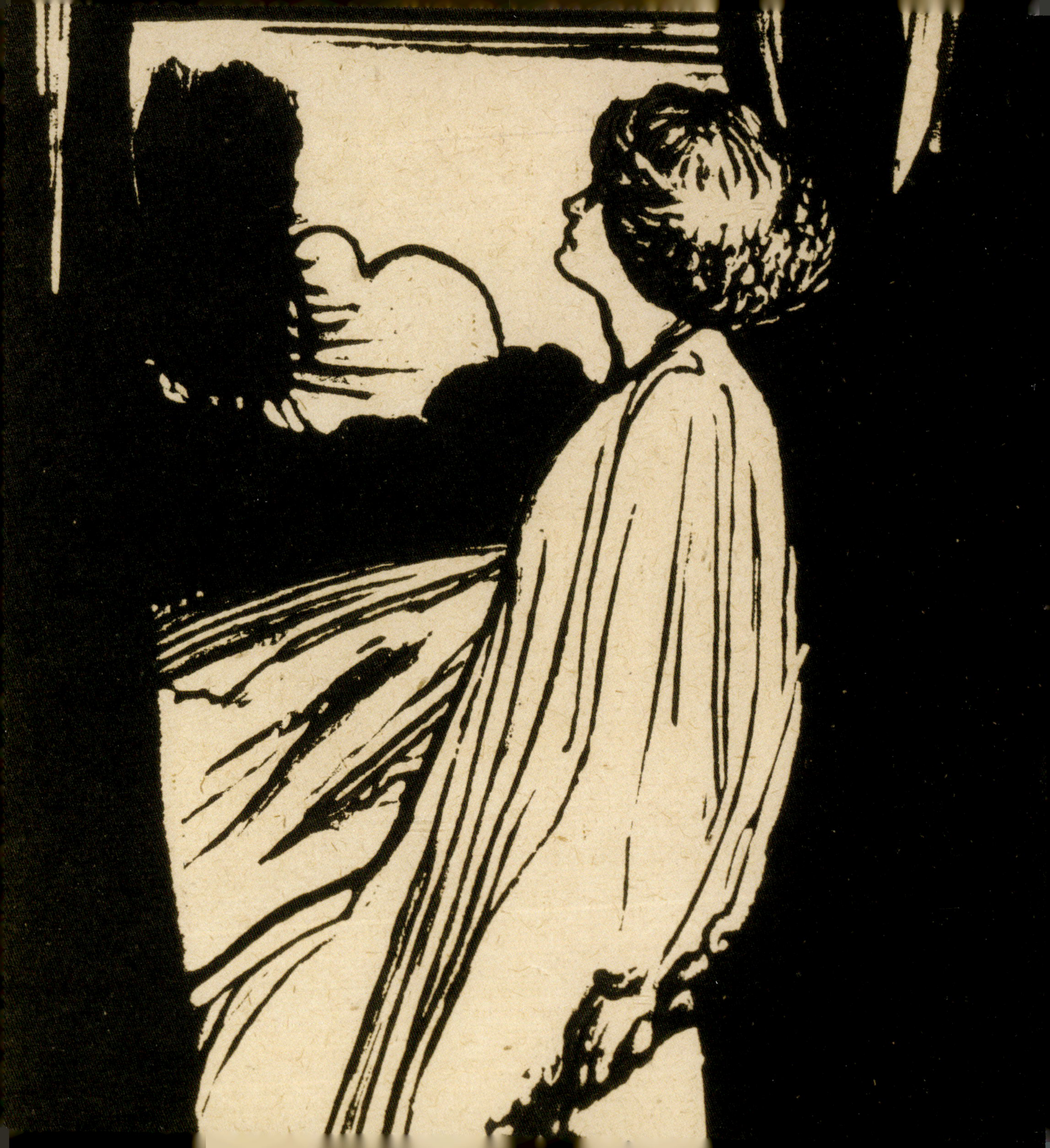

ELLEN TERRY
The Painter's Actress

Veronica Franklin Gould
Keremi Gawade

WATTS GALLERY

First published by Watts Gallery on the occasion of the exhibition
Ellen Terry: The Painter's Actress, 10 June - 11 November 2014

Watts Gallery, Down Lane, Compton, Guildford, Surrey, GU3 1DQ
www.wattsgallery.org.uk
Watts Gallery Registered Charity No. 313612

ISBN 978-0-9561022-2-5

Edited by
Dr. Nicholas Tromans, Brice Curator, Watts Gallery
and
Rhian Addison, Assistant Curator, Watts Gallery

Designed by
Kerris Kaya, Marketing Assistant, Watts Gallery

Front cover: Julia Margaret Cameron, *Ellen Terry*, also known as *Sadness,* 1864. Photograph. Smallhythe Place, National Trust
Back cover: G.F. Watts, *Choosing* (detail), 1864, oil on canvas, National Portrait Gallery
Endpapers: William Nicholson, *Ellen Terry in the roles she played between 1856-1906*, 1906. Lithograph, Smallhythe Place, National Trust
Frontispiece: Edward Gordon Craig, *Ellen Terry as Ophelia* (detail), 1896. Woodcut. Smallhythe Place, National Trust.

CONTENTS

ACKNOWLEDGEMENTS

Susanna Mayor of Smallhythe Place
Nicola Byrne of Smallhythe Place
Maurice Dalton
Paul Meredith
Aurea Carter
Helen Craig
Colin Ford
Sir Michael Holroyd
Diana Houghton
Sir Jack Leslie
Tim Lindholm
Michael Meredith
Leonée Ormond
Richard Ormond

Lenders and Sponsors
The Paul Mellon Centre for Studies in British Art
Marc Fitch Fund
The National Portrait Gallery
Smallhythe Place, National Trust
James Hervey-Bathurst, Eastnor Castle
Louise and Hans van Tartwijk-Novey

Supporters of Staff Positions
The Paul Mellon Centre
The Deborah Loeb Brice Foundation
John Beale

and all those who wish to remain anonymous

FOREWORD

Perdita Hunt, Director, Watts Gallery

Ellen Terry, The Painter's Actress is an opportunity to discover a famous Victorian heroine through a different lens. In keeping with Watts Gallery Trust's efforts to throw a new light upon the nineteenth century through the Watts perspective, this book and exhibition offer a fresh look on a familiar topic.

For obvious reasons Ellen's profile at Watts Gallery has been low. It is therefore exciting and timely for us to celebrate Watts's first wife in this innovative and insightful way by offering a study of images of Ellen. This befits an art gallery, is a refreshing alternative to biography and lets the viewer make their own discoveries.

It has been heartening to find that through this exhibition we have found a new partner. The National Trust, through the generous loans from Smallhythe Place, for which we are immensely grateful, has made a vital contribution to this exhibition. We have strengthened our friendship with James Hervey-Bathurst at Eastnor Castle and the National Portrait Gallery who have continued to provide support and advice. Loans from anonymous private collectors have also made this exhibition possible. In our endeavours we have been assisted by theatre and photography historians who know and admire Julia Margaret Cameron's famous images of Ellen.

We are above all grateful to the authors of this book. Veronica Franklin Gould is a longstanding collaborator of Watts Gallery and a leading Watts specialist. Her epic biography of Watts was published for his centenary in 2004. Here Veronica now adds more to the story with her lively essay on Ellen and Watts. Our gratitude also goes to Keremi Gawade, a scholar specialising in the history of fashion and photography whose original essay we are delighted to be publishing.

We are indebted to the Paul Mellon Centre for Studies in British Art and the Marc Fitch Fund who helped to fund this publication. I am also grateful to The Brice Curator at Watts Gallery, Dr Nicholas Tromans and his team for delivering this book to accompany our exhibition, *Ellen Terry, The Painter's Artist*. His scholarship, enthusiasm and tenacity bring together a celebration and a first in our rediscovery of this giant of the Victorian stage.

This show is the latest in an increasingly ambitious exhibitions programme that has truly made Watts Gallery a centre for the study of Victorian art, design and social history: all of these things are present in this exhibition which we hope you will enjoy along with the other exhibitions that we will be presenting in the future.

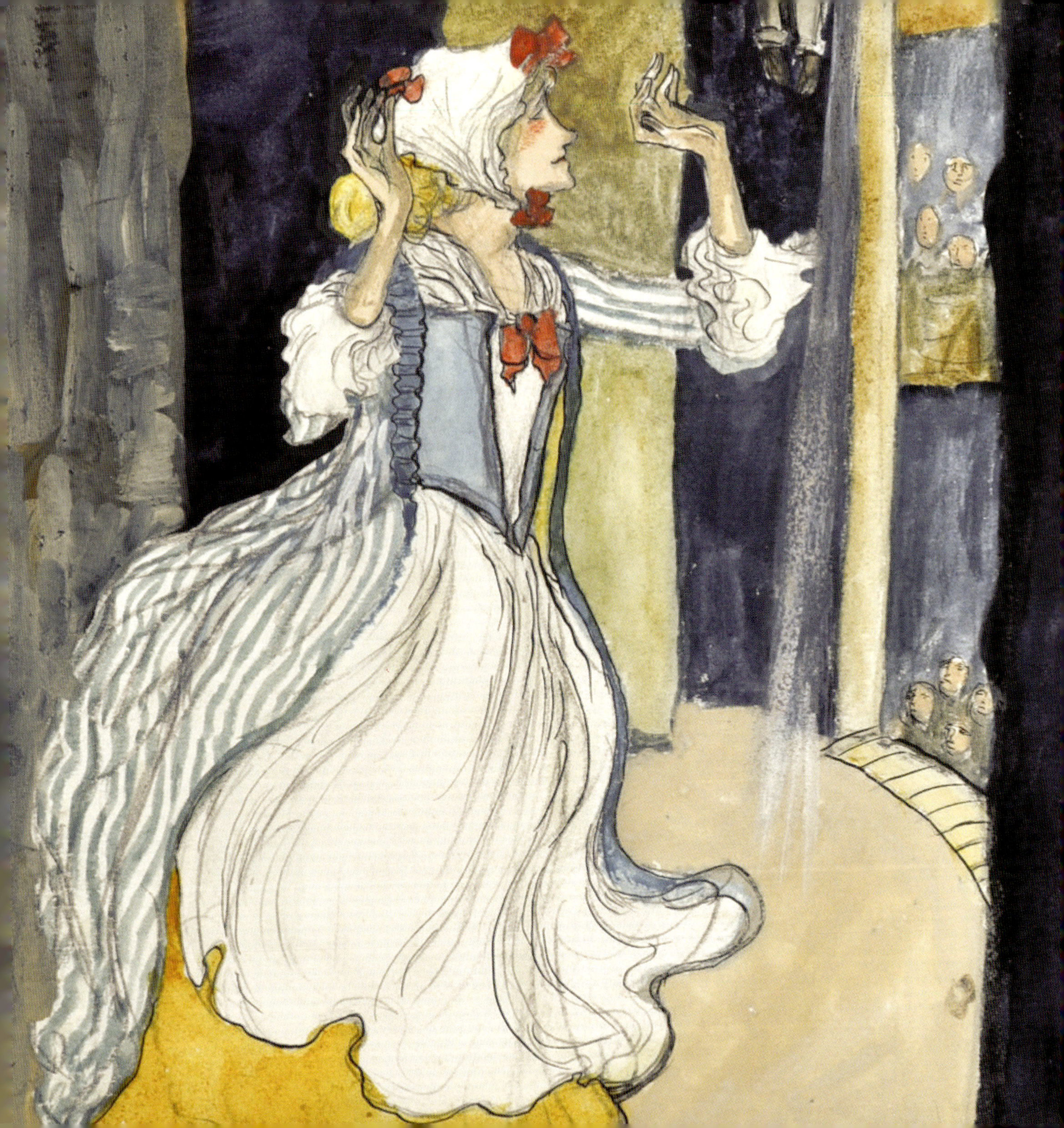

INTRODUCTION

Nicholas Tromans, Brice Curator, Watts Gallery

We are increasingly becoming aware of the creative role of sitters and models in the making of great pictures. Perhaps misled by the use of such laddish terms as 'stunners' (thanks to the Pre-Raphaelites), it used to be hard to see women in nineteenth-century art and photography as more than passive specimens of natural beauty. But few today would dismiss Elizabeth Siddall or Jane Morris in these terms: their allure and charisma were inseparable from their personalities and talents. The case of the great actress Ellen Terry is rather different, in that no-one has ever had cause to doubt her fabulous dramatic talents. Her presence on the stage was felt to be something almost supernatural. Yet as this book, and the exhibition which it accompanies, make clear, Terry was also hugely skilled at helping to create strikingly powerful static images.

As one of the most frequently portrayed women in history – and perhaps the single most photographed woman of the nineteenth century – Terry certainly had plenty of experience, and learned early how to help a photographer or painter create something special. We can be sure that the artists and

Opposite: (Figure 1) Pamela Colman Smith, *Ellen Terry as Nance Oldfield*, 1900. Watercolour, ink, graphite, gouache. Smallhythe Place, National Trust.

Above: (Figure 2) G F Watts, *Ellen Terry with loose hair*, c. 1864. Pencil on paper. Watts Gallery

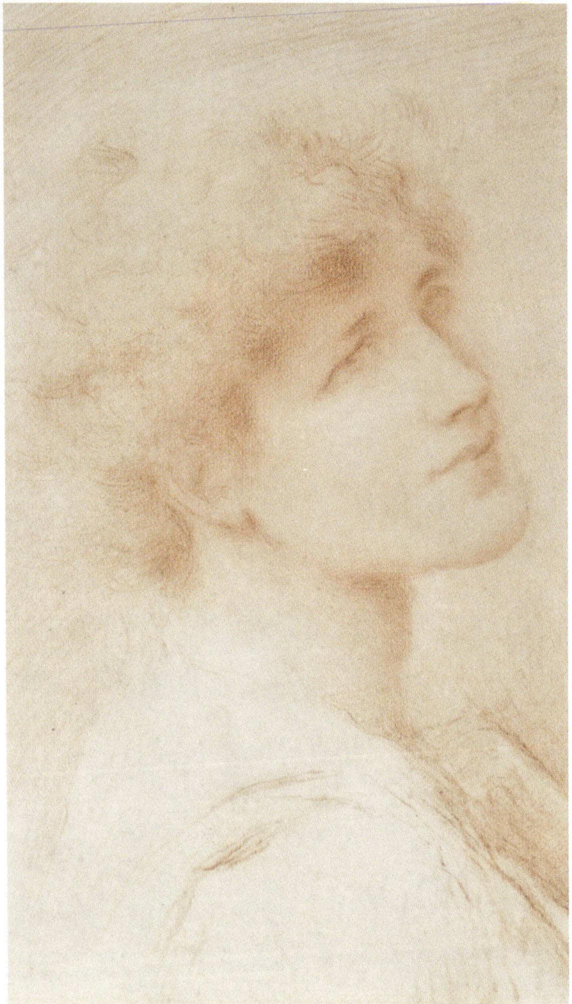

Above: (Figure 3) Simeon Solomon, *Ellen Terry* (detail), date unknown. Sanguine chalk on paper. Smallhythe Place, National Trust

Opposite: (Figure 4) Aristide Fontana, *Ellen Terry as Portia in 'The Merchant of Venice'*, 1880. White marble. Smallhythe Place, National Trust

photographers whose work is reproduced here had the ambition of directing her – of themselves taking up the role of Henry Irving, the great actor-manager whom Terry partnered so successfully for many years at the Lyceum Theatre. But like Irving, they would have found that she had her own ideas as to how she was to be represented; and, again like Irving, they would have seen that her opinions in this area were based on deep knowledge of colour, composition and pictorial rhetoric. She had much more to contribute to these images than simply making sure her 'good side' was given preference.

Terry's thorough understanding of art is intimately connected to her personal history, for the two great loves of her life were also her two great teachers in this field – the painter G. F. Watts and the architect E. W. Godwin. The relationship between Watts and Terry has sometimes been considered a touchy subject. They were married, it seems, as a result of his wishing to rescue a soulful and brilliant girl from the temptations of a life on the stage. When they tied the knot in February 1864 he was 46 and she a little short of her seventeenth birthday. Among the many who have offered opinions on the match over the years, it may be wise to give attention to what was said about it by the artist and collector W. Graham Robertson, who was both a close friend of Terry's and a staunch supporter of Watts Gallery. Robertson felt that Watts had been less than wise in believing himself able to mould so strong a spirit as Terry's already was. But he also wrote that 'It is curious that Watts, who apparently understood her so little, should have painted by far the truest

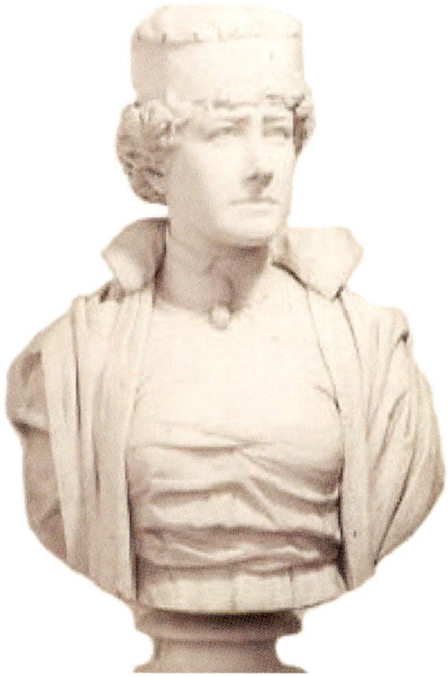

portraits of Ellen Terry', which is praise indeed given the scale of the competition, which included the several portraits that Robertson himself made of his friend over a period of many years.

In this book, Veronica Franklin Gould, the biographer of Watts, offers a generous account of the marriage as a short-lived but profoundly creative engagement which informed the art of each for years to come. Watts was inspired by Terry to paint not only pictures of her of the stature of *Choosing* (Figure 17) and *Watchman, what of the night?* (Figure 11) – two beautiful masterpieces of Victorian narrative portraiture – but also symbolic works, such as *Love and Life* (Figure 19), in which his feelings for her were sublimated into icons of the artist's philosophy. For her part, Terry was ever magnanimous in recognising what she had learned from her first husband and how useful it had been to her career, despite the pain of their early separation. Equally, the man with whom she set up home after her separation from Watts, Godwin, was able to introduce her to many of the principles of the Aesthetic movement in architecture and design.

As Keremi Gawade demonstrates in the essay she has contributed to this book, these lessons in art and design were applied by Terry when presenting – or 'fashioning' – her photographic image. Using a broad range of contemporary journalism as a source for her research, Keremi has been able to explain much of the appeal of what were often mass-produced photographs of Terry in the form of *cartes-de-visite* or 'cabinet cards' – images so ubiquitous as to have later become almost invisible period furniture. Terry clearly managed to convey in these photographs a powerful hybrid of theatre, art and fashion, and a fascinating blending of the public and the private woman, offering vivacious possibilities to the countless admirers and collectors of her photographic portraits.

We would like to think that this book, and the accompanying exhibition, completes the reconciliation of Ellen Terry and G. F. Watts – a reconciliation which, as Veronica Franklin Gould shows, was begun a few years after their formal divorce in 1877. Both Watts and Terry were absolutely devoted to their art; that they were able to give each other so much that enhanced that art is something worth celebrating.

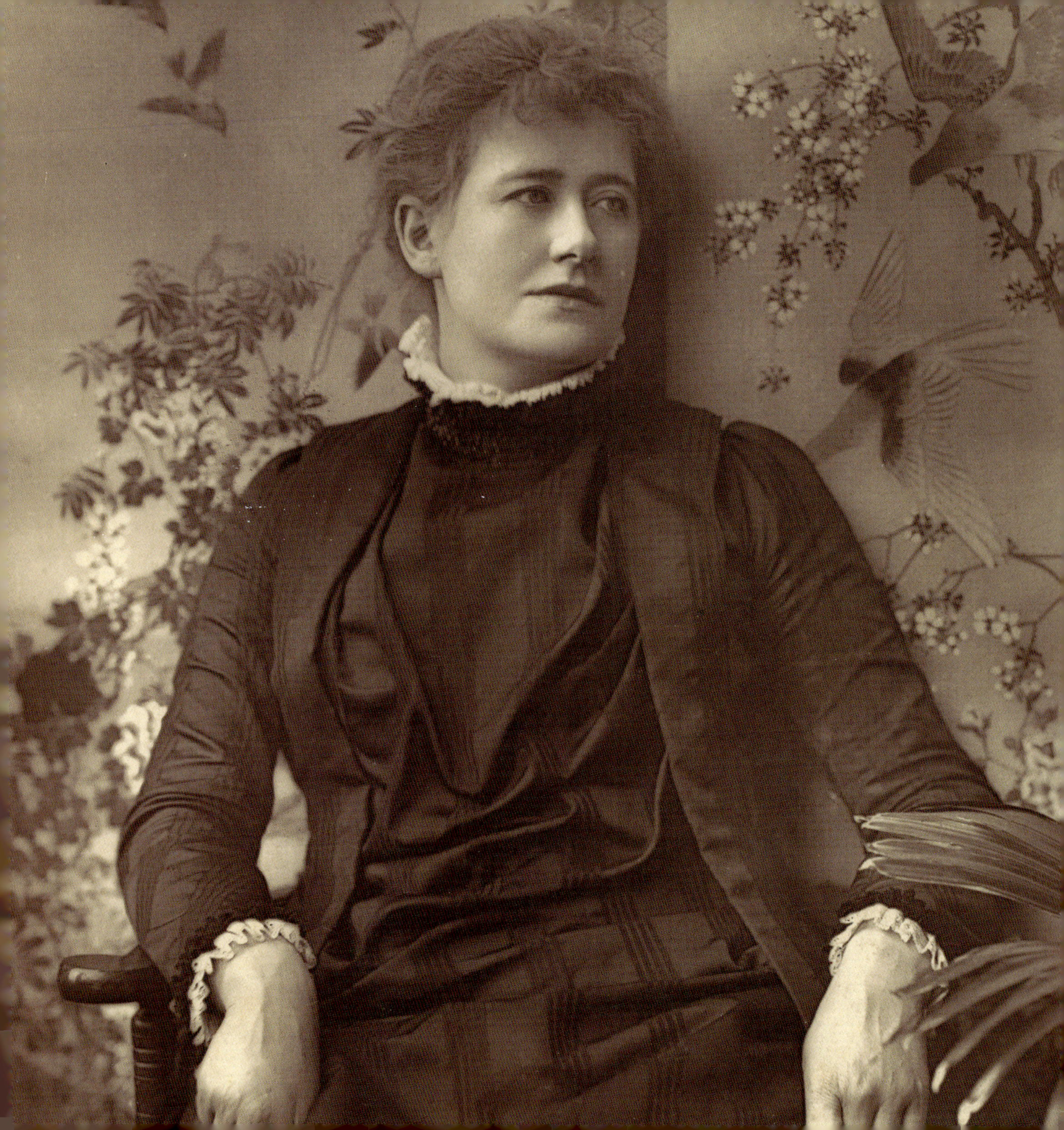

ELLEN TERRY: THE PAINTER'S ACTRESS

Veronica Franklin Gould

'I say', exclaimed the artist John Singer Sargent the moment Ellen Terry appeared as Lady Macbeth in chain armour of iridescent beetle wings. The 41-year-old actress was at the height of her powers in her stage partnership at London's Lyceum Theatre with the actor-manager Sir Henry Irving. As king and queen of the theatre, they blazed a path across England, America and beyond.

Dame Ellen Terry touched audiences differently. Growing up in the age of melodrama, she brought natural performance to the fore. She radiated energy, charm and pathos. Through association with painters, poets and leaders of the Aesthetic Movement – Edward William Godwin, William Burges, James Abbott McNeill Whistler, Oscar Wilde, Alfred, Lord Tennyson, Dante Gabriel Rossetti, Sir Edward Coley Burne-Jones, Sir Lawrence Alma-Tadema and George Frederic Watts were all within her circle – Terry brought to the stage supreme artistic qualities and understanding of the vicissitudes of human life. Especially influential were her relationships with the architect Godwin, the father of her children, and Watts, her first husband, whose art the young Terry transformed. Such was her creative power and his household constraints, that the Terry-Watts marriage would explode within months. But separately, their art and life transformed, each went on to achieve phenomenal international fame.

Watts became a Royal Academician (1867), the subject of unprecedented retrospective exhibitions, the first living painter to be celebrated at the Metropolitan Museum in New York, and an inaugural recipient of King Edward VII's Order of Merit (1902). In the 1890s, he donated his portraits of the Victorian elite to the National Portrait Gallery, and his major Symbolist paintings – their metamorphic drama inspired by his teenage wife – to launch the National Gallery of British Art (Tate). Terry, her pose and movement heightened with harmonious beauty learned in Watts's studio, her Aesthetic dress inspiring fashion, rose to become the transcendent Shakespearean actress, upon whom Sir Henry Irving,

Opposite: (Figure 5) Herbert Rose Barraud, *Dame Ellen Terry seated in front of a decorative screen*, c.1890. Photographic paper on card mount. Smallhythe Place, National Trust

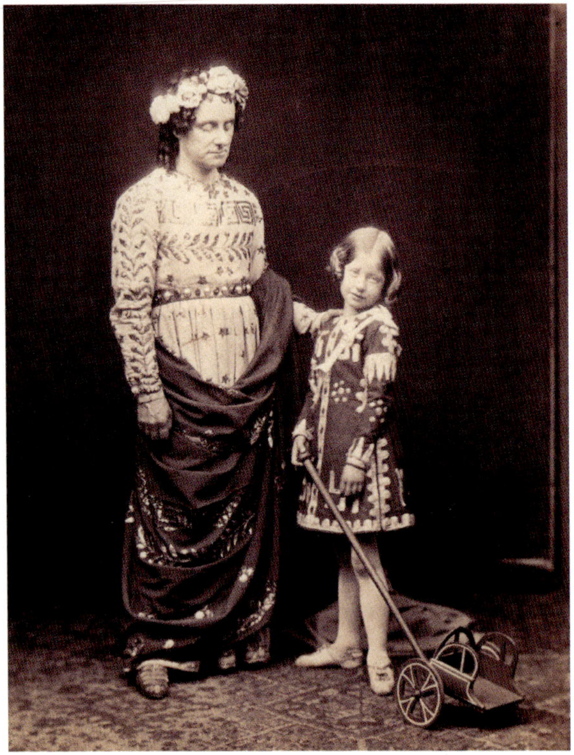

her manager and co-star at the Lyceum Theatre, relied for artistic guidance.

Alice Ellen Terry was born in theatrical lodgings in Coventry on 27 February 1847, the second daughter of Benjamin and Sarah Terry, who were strolling players from Portsmouth, and who instilled their children with grace of movement and perfect diction. They founded a theatrical dynasty, seven of their nine children becoming involved with the theatre. Kate, their eldest and first romantic star to turn men's heads – captivating the novelist Charles Dickens with her womanly tenderness – gave up the stage for marriage.[1] Ellen was their second surviving child. Terry's own son Edward Gordon Craig revolutionised international theatre design. Her great-nephew was the legendary twentieth-century actor Sir John Gielgud.

So precocious was Terry's talent that she won her first Shakespearean role at the age of nine, and attracted instant note as the prince Mamillius in *The Winter's Tale* at the Princess's Theatre, performing before Queen Victoria. Royal patronage of Charles Kean, actor-manager of the Princess's, helped to raise the social status of spoken drama. Terry's early years at the Princess's introduced her to the creative arts. Never before had Shakespeare been given such comprehensive historic settings. Kean was transforming the scenic art of the theatre, bringing in the finest experts in classical architecture and archaeology, decorative arts, costume, music and dance to produce a historic, living work of art.

Dress mattered to Terry. She never forgot the red, silver-braided Grecian coat she wore as Mamillius, nor the way her mother combed her sausage curls, very like those worn by her mother in her portrait by Sir Martin Archer Shee, president of the Royal Academy. There is fire in Terry's eyes in one of her first theatre photographs – highly collectable cabinet cards and smaller *cartes-de-viste* – taken by Martin Laroche. In a better-known image (Figure 6) she stands in balletic pose beside Kean, her head inclined and holding her property cart, its design based on a Greek vase. Her vivacious precocity was noted by the

Times critic, Tom Taylor and 24-year-old Oxford don Charles Lutwidge Dodgson, aka 'Lewis Carroll'.[2] Over the next three years, Mrs Kean – the actress Ellen Tree – impressed the spirit of each part on her young namesake, provoking the child to ignite a sense of real pain and emotion on stage. As well as her 'heart-touching pathos', critics noted artistic contrasts in her acting: 'great sweetness, clearness of enunciation, and delicate light and shade ... the pride, the terror, and the love'. These she learned to imagine and magnify.[3]

It was while performing in Bristol in 1862 that Terry came under the wing of the architect Edward William Godwin, then secretary of the local Shakespeare society. She learned 'to observe, to feel the splendour of things, to *aspire!*' Godwin designed and helped her to make her 'first lovely dress', a Greek-style chiton, to wear as Titania for the opening of the Theatre Royal in Bath on 4 March 1863. So sensual were its figure-hugging folds that she was not allowed to wear the chiton, but Terry had learned to value the historicity of costume and its beauty of line.[4]

On her return to the Haymarket Theatre Royal in London, Terry was seen to have matured into 'one of the happiest specimens of ... the ingénue'. Neither conventional nor affected, her performance in *The Little Treasure* as a boisterous, kindly, impulsive young girl – almost herself, in fact – was seen as being as 'natural, free and uncontrolled as her long back-hair', while her first Shakespearean starring role as Desdemona in *Othello* at the Princess's marked 'an important step in her upward progress'.[5] Meanwhile, Kate's love scenes as Charles Fechter's leading lady at the Lyceum had attracted the attention of G. F. Watts. Keen to paint her portrait, the artist was intrigued too by reports of Ellen. It was probably in late October 1863 that, as chaperone to Kate, Terry first met Watts. The actress marvelled at his studios in the Anglo-Indian home of Thoby and Sara (née

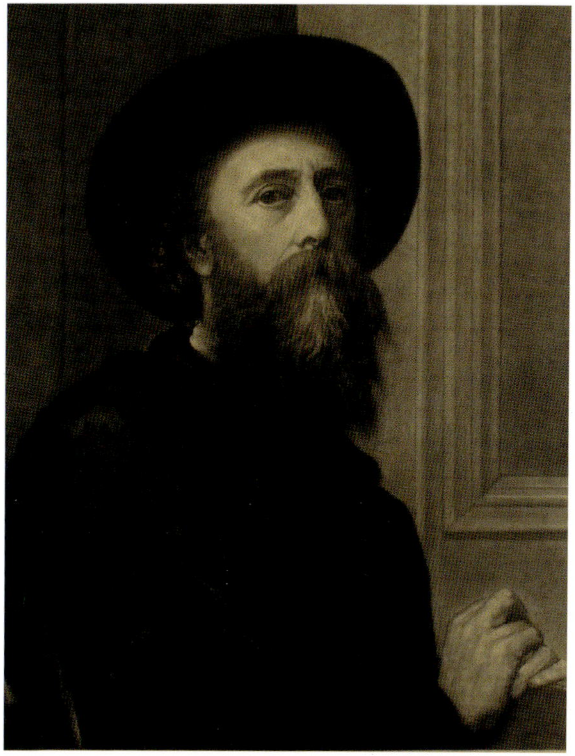

Opposite: (Figure 6) Martin Laroche, *Charles John Kean and Ellen Terry as Leontes and Mamillius in 'The Winter's Tale'*, 26 April 1856. Salt print. National Portrait Gallery

Above: (Figure 7) Charles W. Campbell after G F Watts, *Self-portrait* (1864), date unknown. Engraving. Watts Gallery

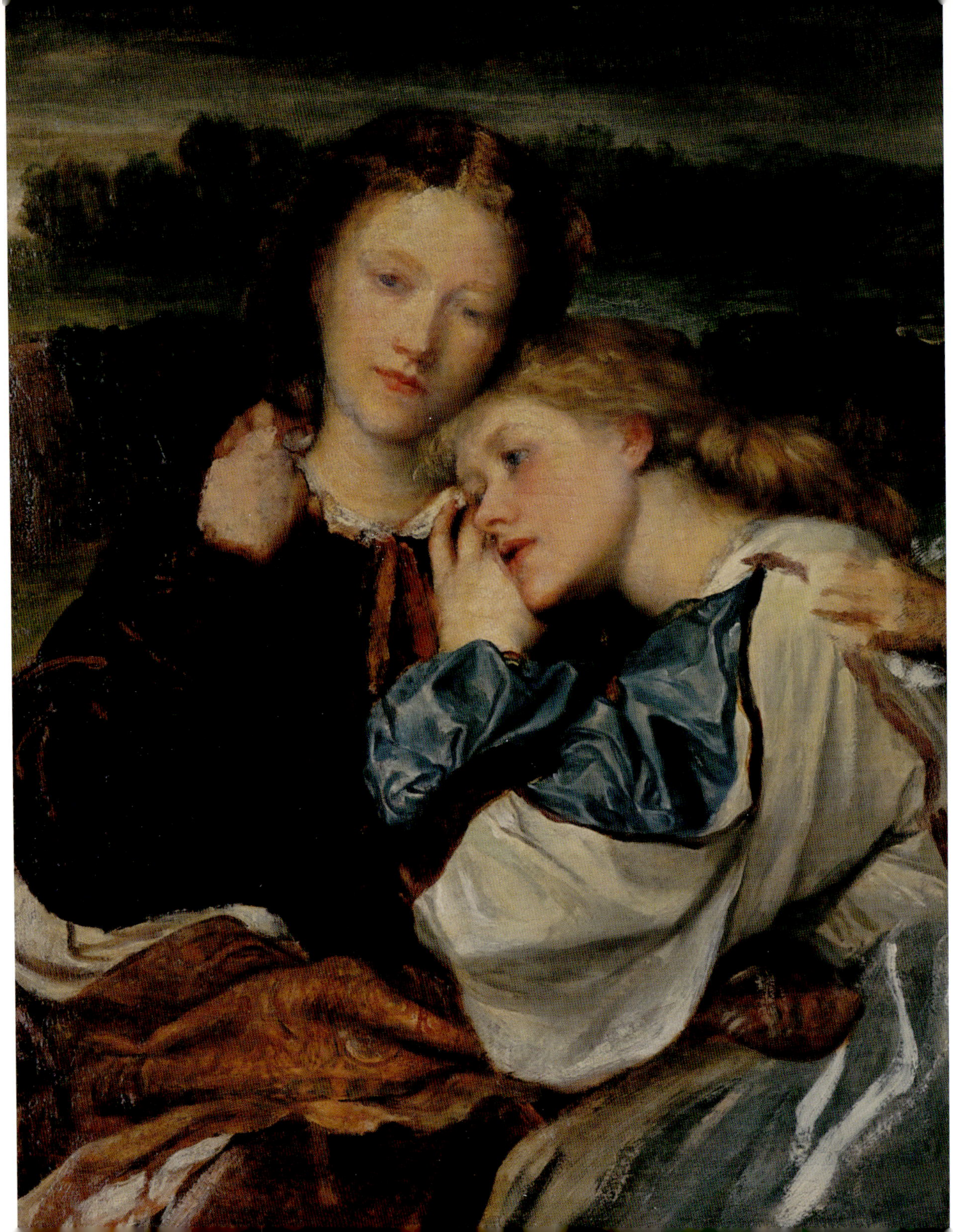

Pattle) Prinsep. Little Holland House in Kensington was not unlike a stage, with frescoes featuring Sara and her sisters in Elgin Marbles poses. Sensationally exotic, the women seemed to materialise out of the backdrop, dressed in loose velvet robes, long pearl necklaces and golden bangles that combined modern Parisian art, Renaissance draperies and Oriental spice, quite unlike the corsets and crinolines of fashion. 'Signor', as they called Watts, appeared in crimson robes in his 1853 self-portrait, *A Venetian Senator,* which hung outside his studio.[6]

Watts painted a double portrait of *The Sisters* (Figure 8) and made Terry its star. Honoured to pose for Signor, she became absorbed in her role for Art. Her eyes and mouth express the intensity she brought to the stage; her golden hair, Titianesque costume and paisley shawl dominate the picture, which Watts set in a Leonardesque landscape to reflect the sisters' journeys as strolling players. Rumour has it that Sara Prinsep saw Kate as a potential wife and muse for Signor, though Kate had little artistic interest and her portrait is unfinished. She appears as a Madonna figure inclining her head with her arm around Terry, who nestles in her shoulder. 'To me the stage seemed a poor place when compared with the wonderful studio where Kate and I were painted as *The Sisters*', Terry recalled. She hand-coloured the photograph of the picture when it was reproduced in her memoirs, noting costume details. Her overdress was of dull white satin, its slashed sleeves edged with brown fur. Deeply affectionate, the girls' pose is more sensual than, but reflects Rossetti's 1862 frontispiece, 'Golden Head by Golden Head', designed for his sister Christina's recently published *Goblin Market and other poems* (Figure 9).

Terry saw Little Holland House as a paradise where all the women were graceful, and all the men were gifted. She posed alone as Joan of Arc – in armour, the heroic quality of which fascinated Watts. So absorbed were artist and sitter that both were surprised when she 'fell all of a heap, nearly fainting' against his painting arm. Their effort to portray heroic vitality unleashed Terry's mystical qualities. Her illuminated face, liquid blue eyes, breastplate and the strands of her hair suggest an inner vision. Watts renamed the picture *Watchman, what of the night?*

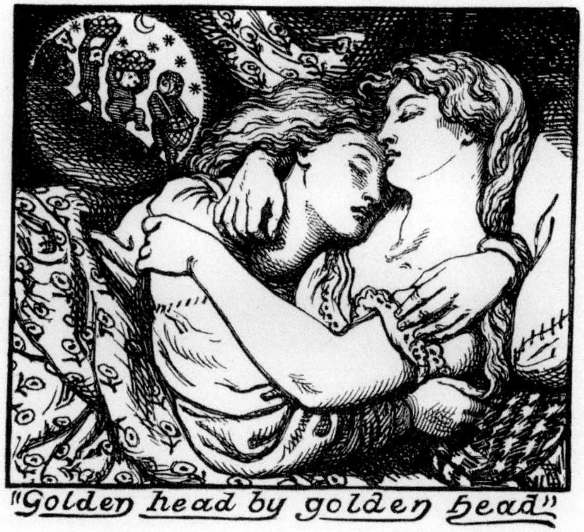

Opposite: (Figure 8) G F Watts, *The Sisters (Kate and Ellen Terry),* 1863. Oil on canvas. Eastnor Castle Collection

Above: (Figure 9) Dante Gabriel Rossetti, Frontispiece for Christina Rossetti's *Goblin Market and Other Poems*, 1862. Private Collection.

(Figure 11). So it is as the watchman in Isaiah's vision of the fall of Babylon that her hands almost wilt with earnestness against her breastplate to express an ambiguous response: 'The morning cometh, and also the night: if ye will enquire, enquire ye: return, come'.[7] Watts's assistant Emilie Barrington later insisted that 'it was not Isaiah, but the dramatic genius of his sitter influencing the artist's imagination in a psychic manner, which made the work ... a quite inspired creation'.[8] Surely, too, Watts had Shakespeare in mind, the prophetic warning of Laertes to his sister Ophelia against losing her heart to Hamlet, the Prince of Denmark, to which his sister, as young and sexually naïve as Terry, replies 'I shall the effect of this good lesson keep / As watchman to my heart.'[9] This most direct visionary painting of Terry exemplifies the imaginative artistic charge between her and Watts, and the excitement each aroused in the other.

The young Greek goddess Persephone was gathering violets and lilies in a meadow, when she was abducted by the god of the underworld and giver of riches. Like Pluto – or so he later tormented himself – Watts lured the ingénue Terry from 'the temptations and abominations' of the stage. He determined to remove her from greenroom taunts and to guide and cultivate her mind for a nobler life in art and society. Blinded by love to the potentially greater difficulty of living without her audience, the artist proposed marriage. He drew her bowing deeply to her audience, as though bidding farewell (Figure 10). 'I was just dreaming of and aspiring after another world, a world full of pictures and music and gentle, artistic people with quiet voices and elegant manners.'

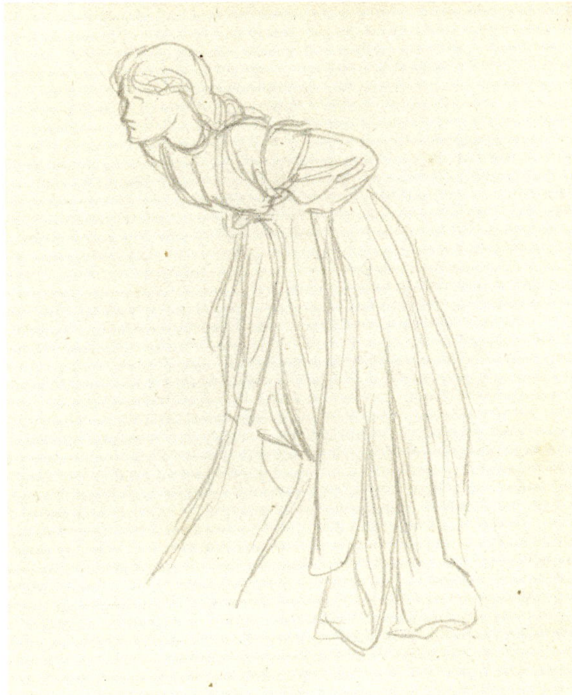

Above: (Figure 10) G F Watts, sketch of Ellen Terry bowing, c. 1863/4. Pencil on paper, from sketch book. Watts Gallery

Opposite: (Figure 11) G F Watts, *Watchman, What of the Night?* c. 1864. Oil on panel. Private Collection

In January 1864, her hormones aflame, the teenager left the stage for immortality on canvas. 'I was in Heaven for I knew I was to live with those pictures. "Always," I thought, and to sit to that gentle Mr W. and clean his brushes, and play my idiotic piano to him.'[10] The thirty-year age difference, if disconcerting, was not unusual in the Victorian era, but Ellen could never be mistress of Little Holland House where Watts

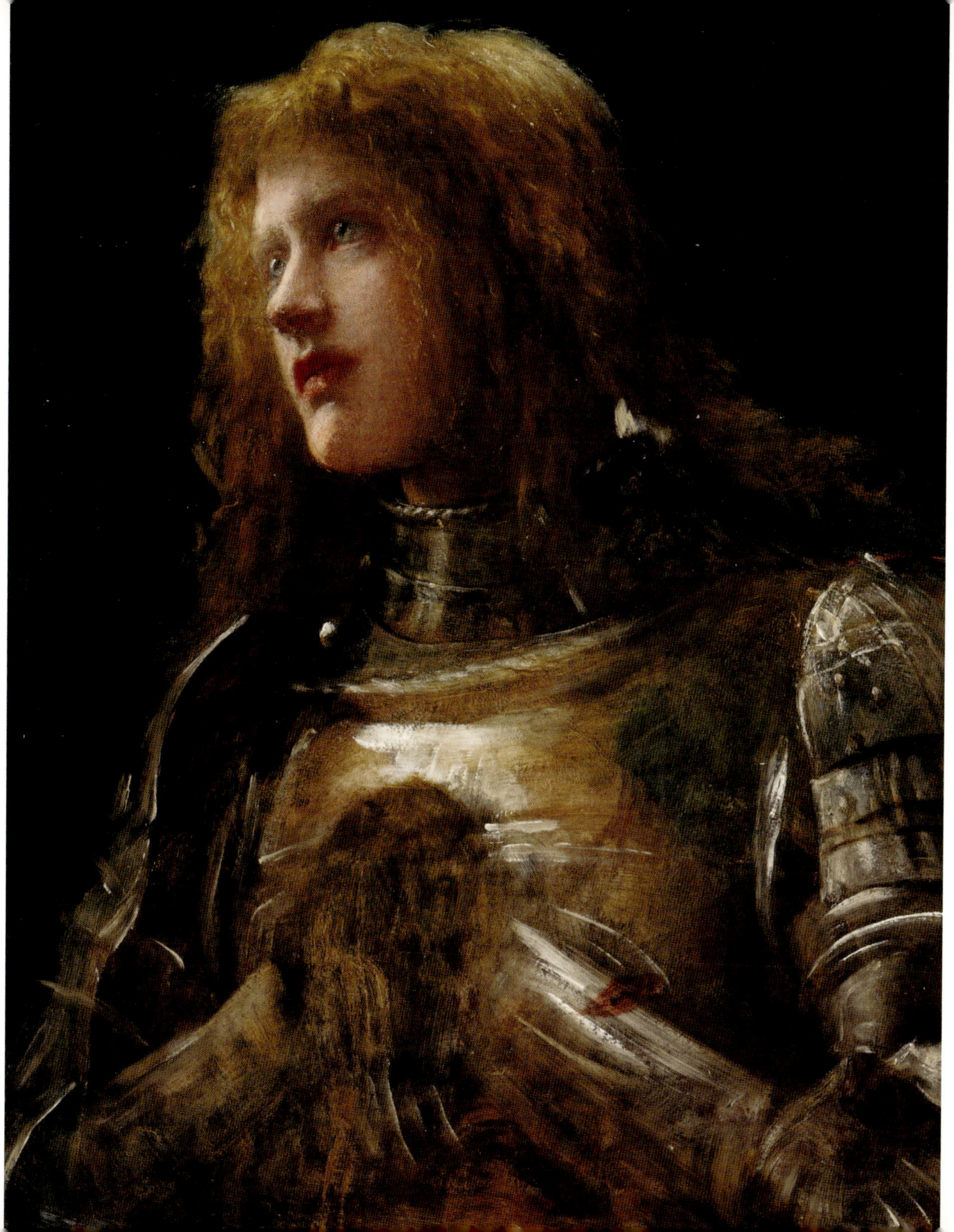

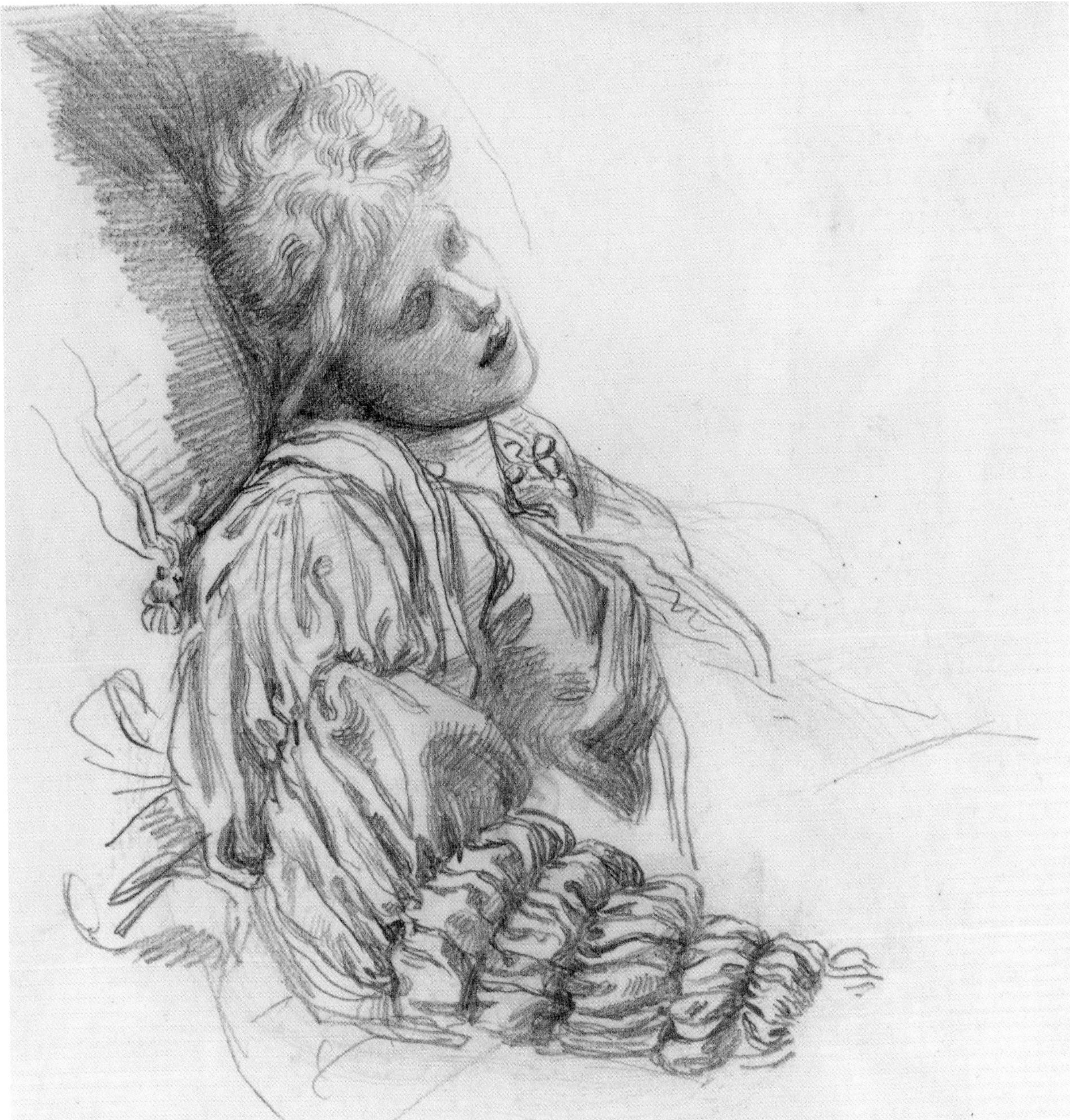

remained a long-term guest of the Prinseps; and there was the stigma of the stage. A theatrical career offered women the rare opportunity to earn their own living, on a par with, or even more than men, but Victorians looked down on professional actors. Even the tragedian William Charles Macready, who strove to elevate the theatre, made his wife give up acting. Socially, Watts and Terry were well matched, neither quite acceptable enough for his flirtatious aristocratic sitters, whom he now asked to help prepare Terry for her role in society.

Both Terry and Watts had trained for their art from childhood, striving to perfect gesture and expression. The artist had honed his skills from the age of ten in the studio of William Behnes, the future Sculptor-in-Ordinary to the Queen. Deserting the Royal Academy Schools to learn directly from old master paintings at the National Gallery and the Elgin Marbles, Watts also travelled to Italy to study the art of fresco. Although he had achieved fame in the Palace of Westminster competitions of 1843 and 1847, the year Terry was born, his career had been controversial. Watts's portraits were highly valued – leaders of the era sat for his historic series – but his vision to inspire the people with metaphysical frescoes had been too avant-garde for British taste. His star was now rising and the Royal Academy was looking to Watts for advice.

It was sensationally mad to marry. Two geniuses of the Victorian era on their climb to fame, both seasoned to observe human nature and with imagination bursting from their souls, might create

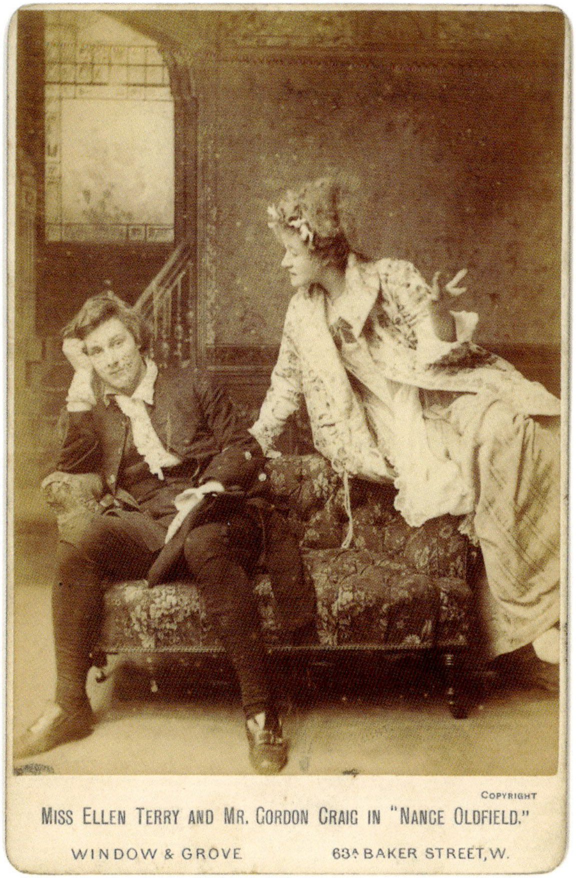

Opposite: (Figure 12) G F Watts, *Ellen Terry asleep*, c. 1864. Pencil on paper. Private Collection

Above: (Figure 13) Window & Grove, *Ellen Terry as Nance in 'Nance Oldfield' with Gordon Craig*, c. 1883. Photograph. National Trust, Smallhythe Place

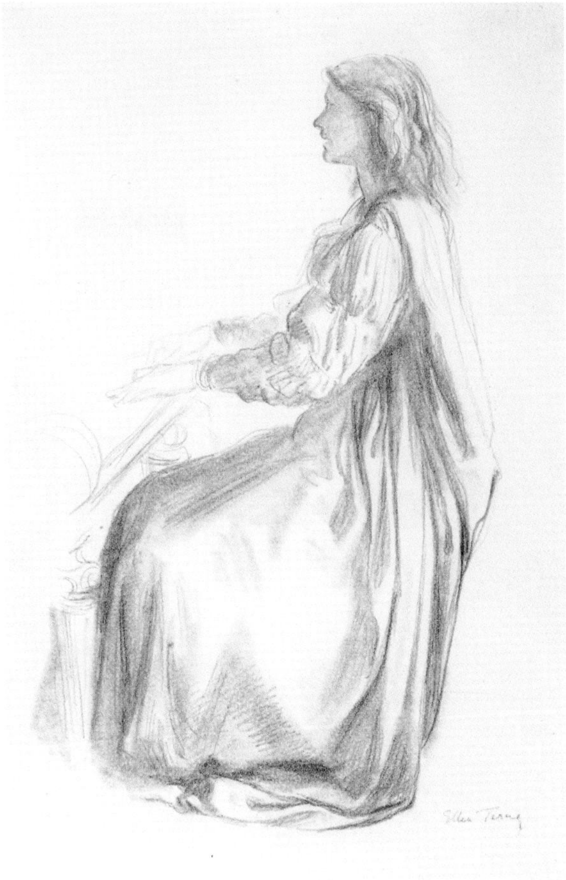

Above: (Figure 14) G F Watts, *Ellen Terry at a piano*, c. 1864. Pencil on paper. Collection of Louise and Hans van Tartwijk-Novey

Opposite: (Figure 15) G F Watts, *Ellen Terry*, c. 1864. Oil on canvas. National Portrait Gallery

compelling pictures together. Could the teenager suppress her exuberance for a quieter role as his wife? Long-limbed, with fair hair and sparkling eyes, Terry rode life like a wild Amazon, recalled her son Gordon Craig, 'always taking leaps in the dark'. The artist William Holman Hunt designed her wedding dress, a Renaissance-style gown of grey-brown silk, the sleeves latticed with black velvet, over which she wore an Indian shawl and quilted white bonnet. Carrying a sprig of orange blossom, Terry danced up the aisle of St Barnabas Church, Kensington, to marry Watts on 20 February 1864. Her tears of joy spoiled the picture for her bridegroom: 'Don't cry', he told her, 'It makes your nose swell.' His depictions of her nose present a perfect line.[11]

On honeymoon, as they celebrated his forty-seventh and her seventeenth birthdays, Watts made delicate drawings of his bride lying in bed asleep (Figure 12), relaxing in bed, stretched out reading and playing the piano. Sara Prinsep's elder sister Julia Margaret Cameron, who looked to Watts for artistic guidance, brought her new large camera and an album of experimental soft-focus photographs. Terry, posing in her bridal gown at Little Holland House, became the first sitter to be photographed by Cameron while Watts painted them. In this rare informal photograph (Figure 16) Terry has lowered one hand to the other, revealing their largeness, which the actress preferred to conceal. She is looking away from the camera, as though the photographer has caught her unawares. Her expression is wary and the pose – if pose it be – is similar to Watts's portrait of his wife at a stage curtain (Figure 15). In the darkroom, Cameron has

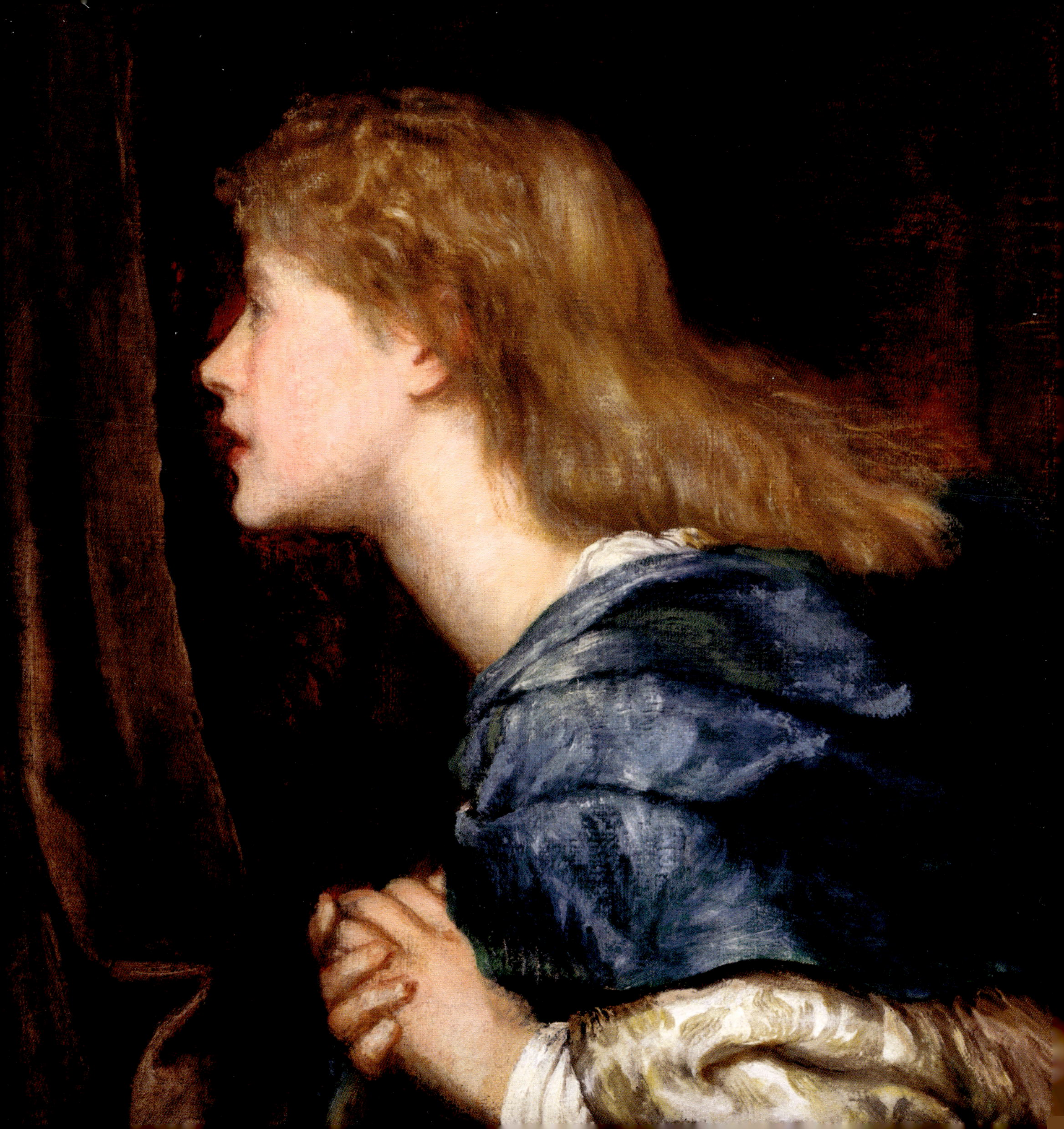

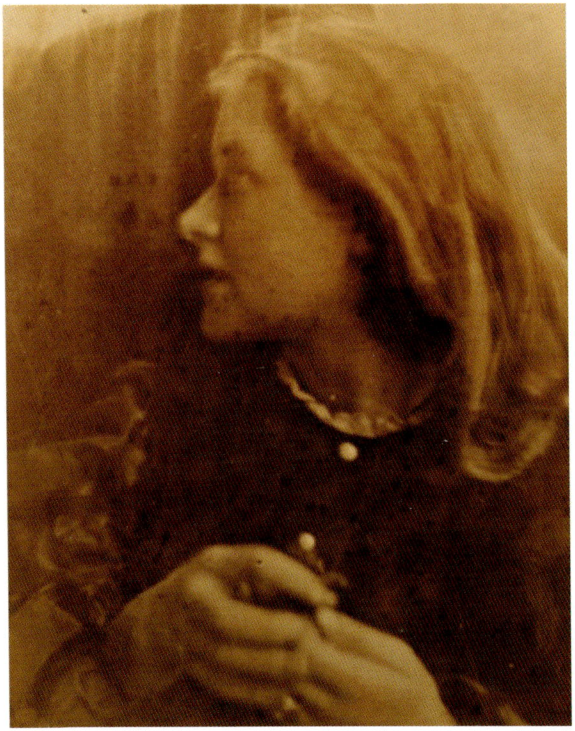

Above: (Figure 16) Julia Margaret Cameron, *Mrs Watts*, 1864. Albumen print. Private Collection

Opposite: (Figure 17) G F Watts, *Choosing*, 1864. Oil on strawboard. National Portrait Gallery

tried to emulate Watts's shading to refine the profile of Terry's jaw, not yet achieving the poetry or pathos of his bridal portrait *Choosing* (Figure 17) or of *Sadness* (Figure 36), the famous photograph she took of Terry a week after their marriage. The actress recorded on her cabinet card that this was taken on her birthday.[12] If so, the gift was mutual. Over the last seven years Terry had posed for hundreds of theatre photographs. The combination of both women's passion for art, the actress's dramatic sensibility, her photographic experience and poignant emotional transformation following her marriage to Watts, resulted in some of 'the most beautiful and remarkable pictures in the history of photography' according to Helmut Gernsheim.[13] Cameron photographed Terry in a deeply reflective pose, dressed in a loose Grecian robe, fingering her necklace – a device to show her wedding rings and suppress her instinct to fidget – and exhibited the image as *Sadness* at medal-winning international displays. To the writer J. B. Priestley, it encapsulated 'Woman herself, her soul withdrawn behind those heavy eyelids, the mystery, the challenge, the torment, the solace'.[14]

Watts made love to his wife in pigment and pencil, tenderly directing her to shape herself into line. Terry's charisma spurred him to produce outstanding, unusually instinctive work. Barrington wondered 'whether he ever realized whence came the inspiration which resulted in his most glorious visions on canvas.'[15] As Watts painted his bride, he taught her to infuse beauty of line with harmony and rhythm. Critics had long marvelled at her grace onstage. Now there would be harmony in each pose and gesture. In her portrait at the stage curtain (Figure 15), her hands clasped and pressed to her shawl, her mouth parted in a more anxious expression than in Cameron's bridal photograph, Terry is truly acting. Tender in spirit, such is the flow of the picture, her 'eager impulsive throat' extended, we can sense her vibrant nature, the nervous athleticism that powered

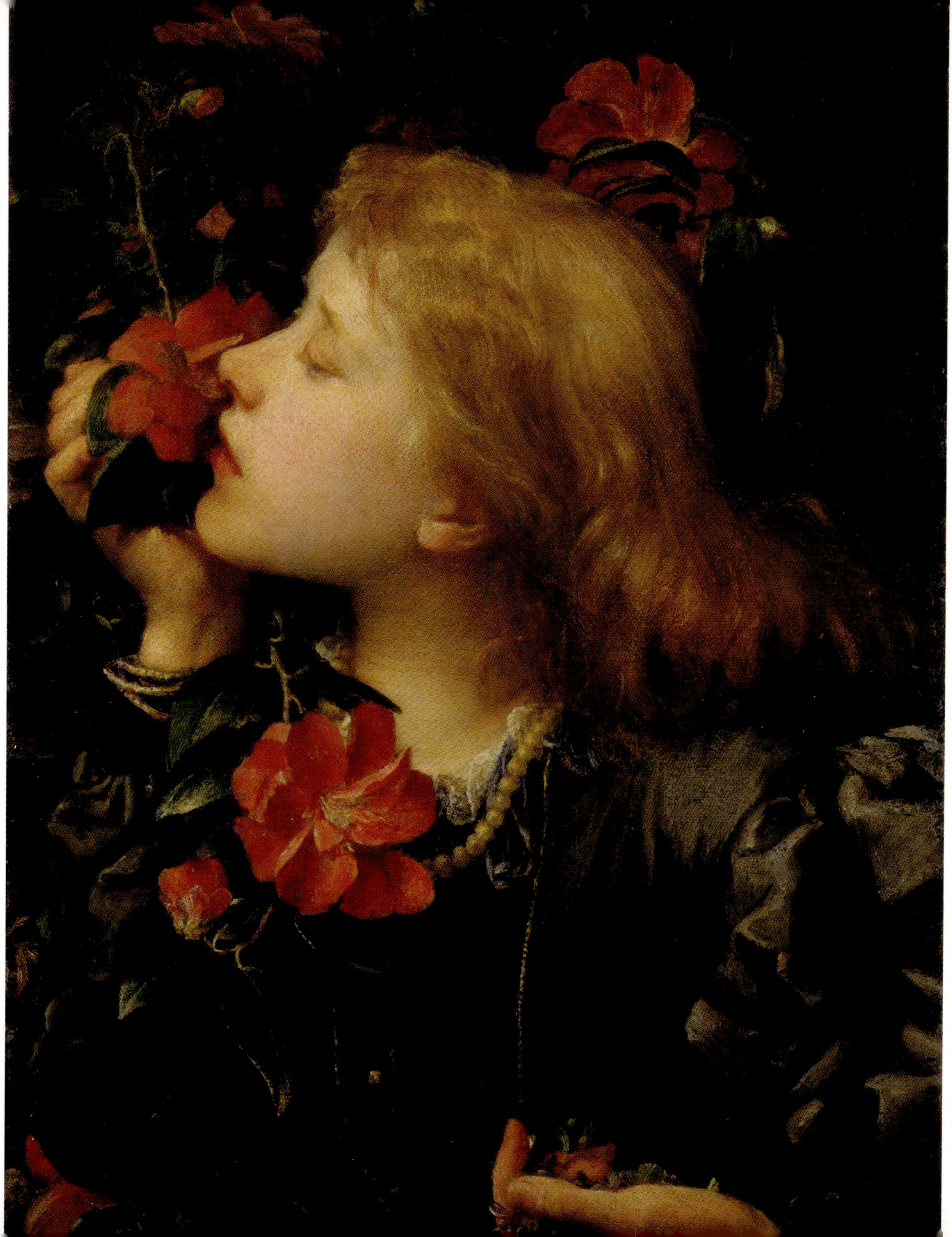

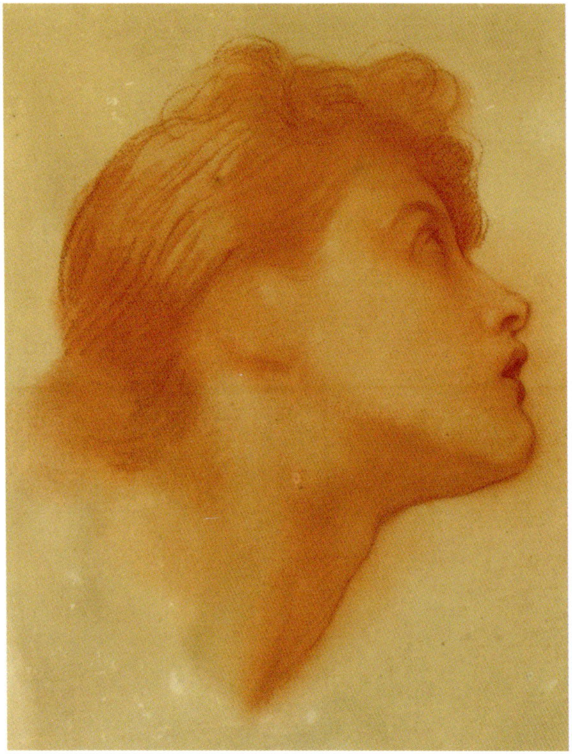

her 'slightly veiled voice' to reach the remotest audiences, created marital challenge, and would transform Watts's imaginative subject painting, but put awful strain on their marriage.[16]

The artist lived for sunrise, for the daylight that enabled him to paint, whereas Terry used to perform long after sundown. Absorbed as she was holding a pose for hours on end to create art, she could not resist teasing, even irritating the artist. Yet she continued to feel that he was glorifying her to artistic stardom. 'I was happy, because my face was the type which the great artist who had married me loved to paint'.[17] Drawing on her theatrical skills, Terry was an inspired model. Watts's sanguine study of her head and neck (Figure 18) stretched further, as she gazed up in wonder – evidence of their harmony in art – would later be taken up for his key universal subject, *Love and Life* (Figure 19).

Choosing (Figure 17) was a triumph at the Royal Academy exhibition in the spring of 1864. Neither before nor afterwards, in an oeuvre of several thousand, did Watts paint a portrait so exquisite. It is a jewel-like Pre-Raphaelite picture, radiant with love. His enchantment is palpable. Terry holds fragrant violets at her heart to represent Love. But at her nose is the showy, scentless camellia, to symbolise the theatre. Camellias bloom all about her. Did the artist add more, doubting that life without performance could satisfy Terry? The violets, a possible allusion to Laertes' warning to Ophelia, may question the durability of his affection:

> For Hamlet and the trifling of his favour,
> Hold it a fashion and a toy in blood,
> A violet in the youth of primy nature,
> Forward, not permanent, sweet, not lasting,
> The perfume and suppliance of a minute;
> No more.[18]

Tom Taylor, reviewing the Academy exhibition for the *Times*, hailed *Choosing* as 'the loveliest example of colour and the most delicate piece of fancy in the exhibition', an exceptional example of the poetry of painting.[19]

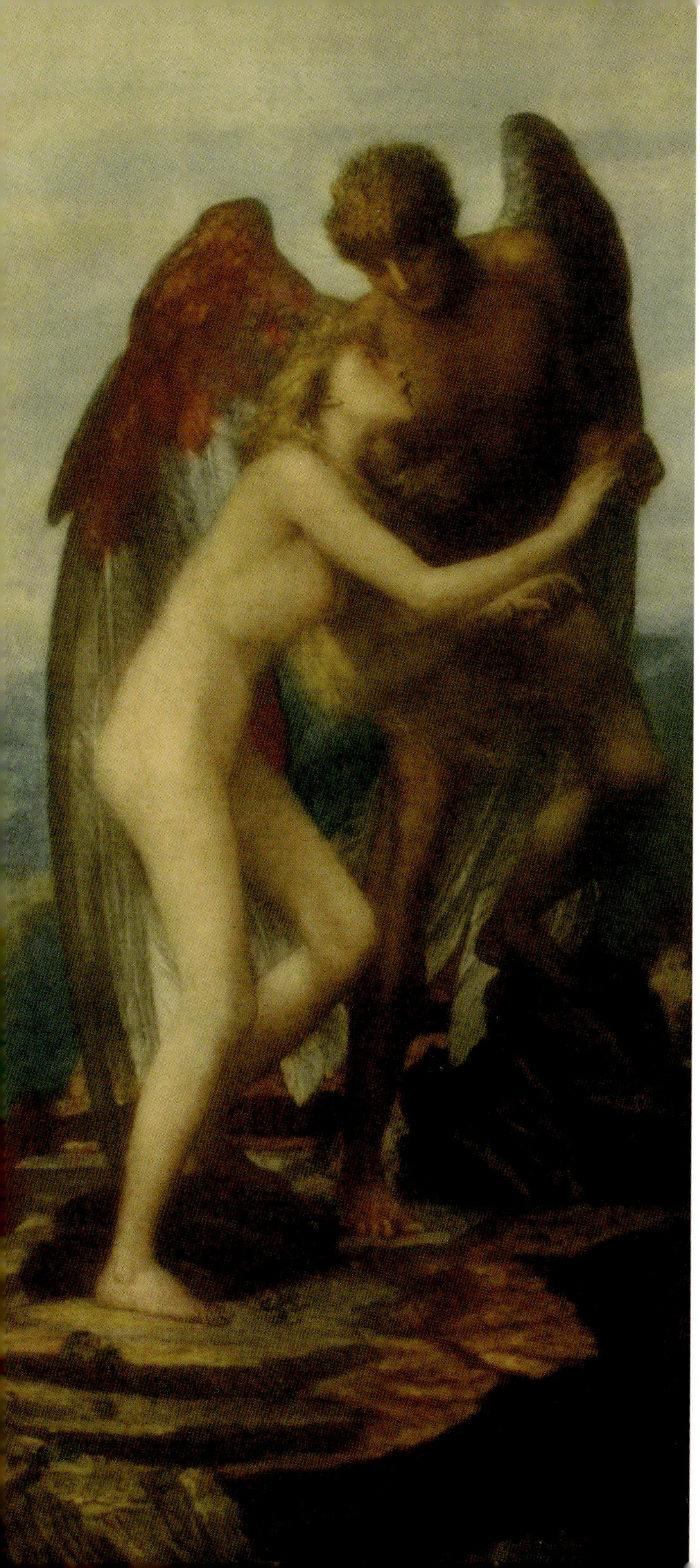

Cameron registered six photographs of Terry in 1864 and five of Watts. In one image of the artist, he is seen arranging the folds of his sleeve as Titian would have done; Terry's shadowy appearance as the *South-West Wind* (Figure 39) has the diagonal structure of Watts's huge painting of *Time and Oblivion*. At her guest cottage near the Tennysons at Freshwater on the Isle of Wight, Cameron took monumental photographs of Terry in *The Opera Box* with a young man (Figure 21), and posing as the Greek slave *Medora*.[20] The poet laureate, who was sitting to Watts, gave her private readings of his poetry.

While Terry did not regret leaving the stage, having to remain silent at Little Holland House inhibited her role as the artist's wife. If she could no longer aspire or respect his coterie, her observations reflect her innate theatrical artistry. She noted how Benjamin Disraeli's daringly bright blue tie and straggly curls shook as he walked, and how William Gladstone, 'like a volcano at rest' had a calm, pale face, calm as the grey crust of Etna. 'You looked into piercing dark eyes and caught a glimpse of the red-hot crater beneath the crust'. She preferred the poet laureate's rough simplicity to the society coat and manners of Robert Browning.[21] Her views reflect Watts's ambition for portraiture – to depict the mind of the sitter – as well as her own instinct for texture and movement that could be, at times, volcanic.

Opposite: (Figure 18) G F Watts, *Study for the figure in 'Love and Life',* 1880s. Chalk on paper. Watts Gallery

Left: (Figure 19) Emery Walker after G F Watts, *Love and Life* (c. 1884/5), 1913. Photogravure print. Watts Gallery

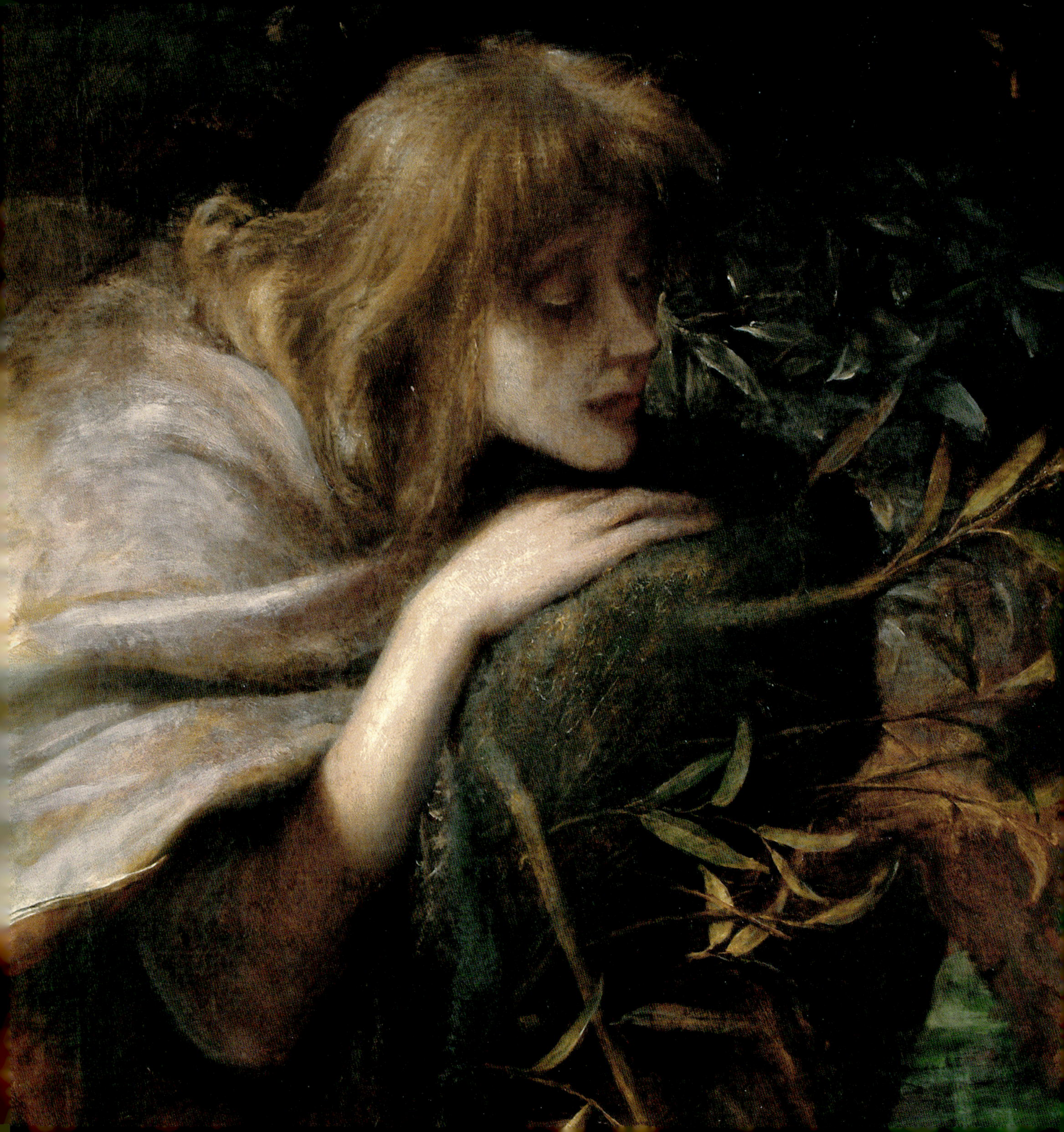

Watts and Terry's most haunting extant collaboration is the painting of *Ophelia* (Figure 20) was very likely undertaken to help override challenges in the Watts marriage. (Kate Terry was appearing in the role at the Lyceum that summer.) Celebrating the 'exquisitely tender pathos' that Terry brought to the stage,[22] she posed as though deranged by ill-fated love for Hamlet in the branches of the 'willow growing aslant a brook', from which she is about to fall to her death, her eyes alert with madness, her fingers splayed. In November 1864, her spirits suppressed, Terry triggered real-life comparisons with Ophelia at Little Holland House. After a night spent away from the house, she was not allowed back. The couple were distraught. Neither wished to separate, but the deed was formalised on 26 January 1865. It was not until after Terry's elopement and break-up with Godwin (their two children were given the surname 'Craig' after the volcanic Scottish island Ailsa Craig) that Terry and Watts were eventually divorced in November 1877 – shortly before her brief marriage to the lesser actor Charles 'Kelly' Wardell. Watts would transform *Ophelia* (Figure 20) for exhibition at the Grosvenor Gallery in 1878.

The partnership of Watts and Terry – two artists seeking their ideal – collapsed, but its legacy would endure and magnify. Terry's emotional impulse transformed Watts's imaginative art, giving it a theatrical metamorphic power. At Little Holland House, Terry had met men of taste and learning, leading artists and poets, who contributed to her appreciation of art and beauty. Posing for Watts unleashed her mystical spirit and imbued her with a sense of harmony that would enchant audiences throughout her stellar career. As her biographer Nina Auerbach put it, 'She found herself as an artist when she flowered as an artist's model; in pictures she was most mercurially and suggestively alive.'[23] Terry inspired and reacted to Watts's brush more than any other sitter. Together they sparked a visionary intensity never before realised in their art.

In despair, Watts began to destroy portraits of his wife. The shipping magnate Eustace Smith MP galloped over to Little Holland House and saved *Choosing* (Figure 17) to inaugurate his avant-garde collection. The actress's favourite painting of herself, it remains one of the National Portrait Gallery's most popular Victorian portraits. Furious at her ejection by Watts, Terry had returned to the family home in Stanhope Street, Euston. The Gothic revival architect William Burges now fed her artistic spirit, designing a decorative book box for her Shakespeare collection. In July 1865 she posed defiantly in her wedding dress for a photograph by Dodgson (Lewis Carroll) (Figure 37), just as *Alice's Adventures in Wonderland* was published. Ironically, she signed the image '*Truly Yours, Ellen Alice Watts*'. 'I hate the word Artist' she wrote to a friend.[24] Watts drew a secret image of himself seated, cross-legged, bent double in despair, with a prayer, which he sent to Terry. That pose, in final female form, would be developed into his iconic Symbolist picture, *Hope* (1886). In the meantime, shutting himself away from society, he made nude

Opposite: (Figure 20) G F Watts, *Ophelia*, c. 1863-80. Oil on canvas. Watts Gallery

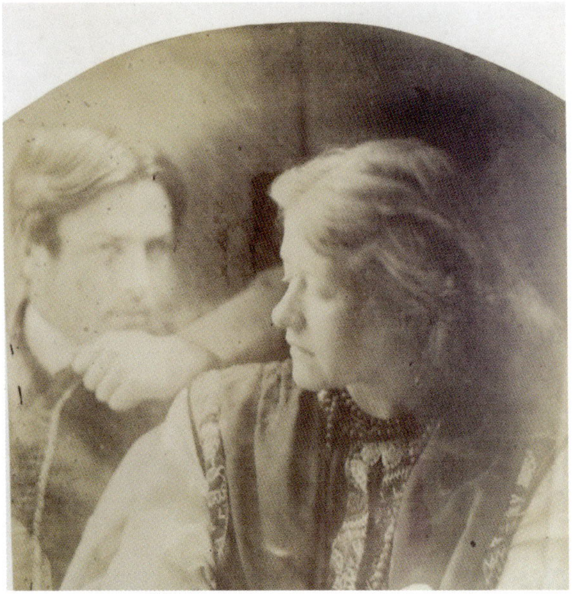

Above: (Figure 21) Julia Margaret Cameron, *The Opera Box* (detail), 1864. Albumen print. Private Collection

Opposite: (Figure 22) Frederic Hollyer after G F Watts, *Wife of Plutus (or Pluto)*, c. 1885. Photograph. Watts Gallery

studies from Mary Bartley, a housemaid as admirably tall as Terry. One oil study of 'Long Mary', cross-legged, her head in her arms, is regarded as the first painted sketch for *Hope* – the artist's idea being that any advance from the depths of despair offers hope.

Love and Life, exhibited at the Academy in 1865, marked a dynamic new direction in the artist's imaginative work. Love with wings of fire was seen dragging a strong man along Life's thorny path.[25] Later, Watts would develop the picture in reverse, giving the fragile figure of Life the face from his sanguine drawing of Terry (Figure 18). Meanwhile, he depicted her and himself together as Dante's forbidden lovers *Paolo and Francesca*, enfolded in each other's arms in the everlasting winds of Hell. Variants of this erotic subject show Francesca with the face of the unattainable women he loved. Uniquely, Terry was portrayed in the nude.[26]

Watts's sensual half-length nude pictures on themes of unfulfilled longing owe much to the Shakespearean inspiration of his wife and the passion of artist and actress. In *The Wife of Pygmalion* he shows Galatea coming to life, as he had wished to cultivate and elevate his own wife; and in Fata Morgana the unattainable temptress flees from the knight. *The Wife of Pluto* (Figure 22) – the antithesis of *Choosing* – shows Persephone, ravished yet unsatisfied, with Terry's golden hair, thrusting her nose towards luxuriant silk drapery shaped like a giant scentless carnation; the jewels were added later to reinforce the artist's protest against 'the dis-ease of wealth'.[27] In *Orpheus and Eurydice* Watts depicted the moment, full of hope, but fatal, when the poet Orpheus, attempting to rescue his wife from the underworld, gazes back at her too soon; he clasps her breast, she falls away, her arms lose their grip, her flesh pales, her head becomes limp and she slips back to oblivion. Her transparent *mouvementé* drapery, contrasting with his vigorous, ruddy body, heightens the sense of desire and the impotence of love in the face of death. Watts's marble bust of *Clytie*, which caused a stir at the Academy in 1868, epitomises Terry's dramatic pathos. The wood-

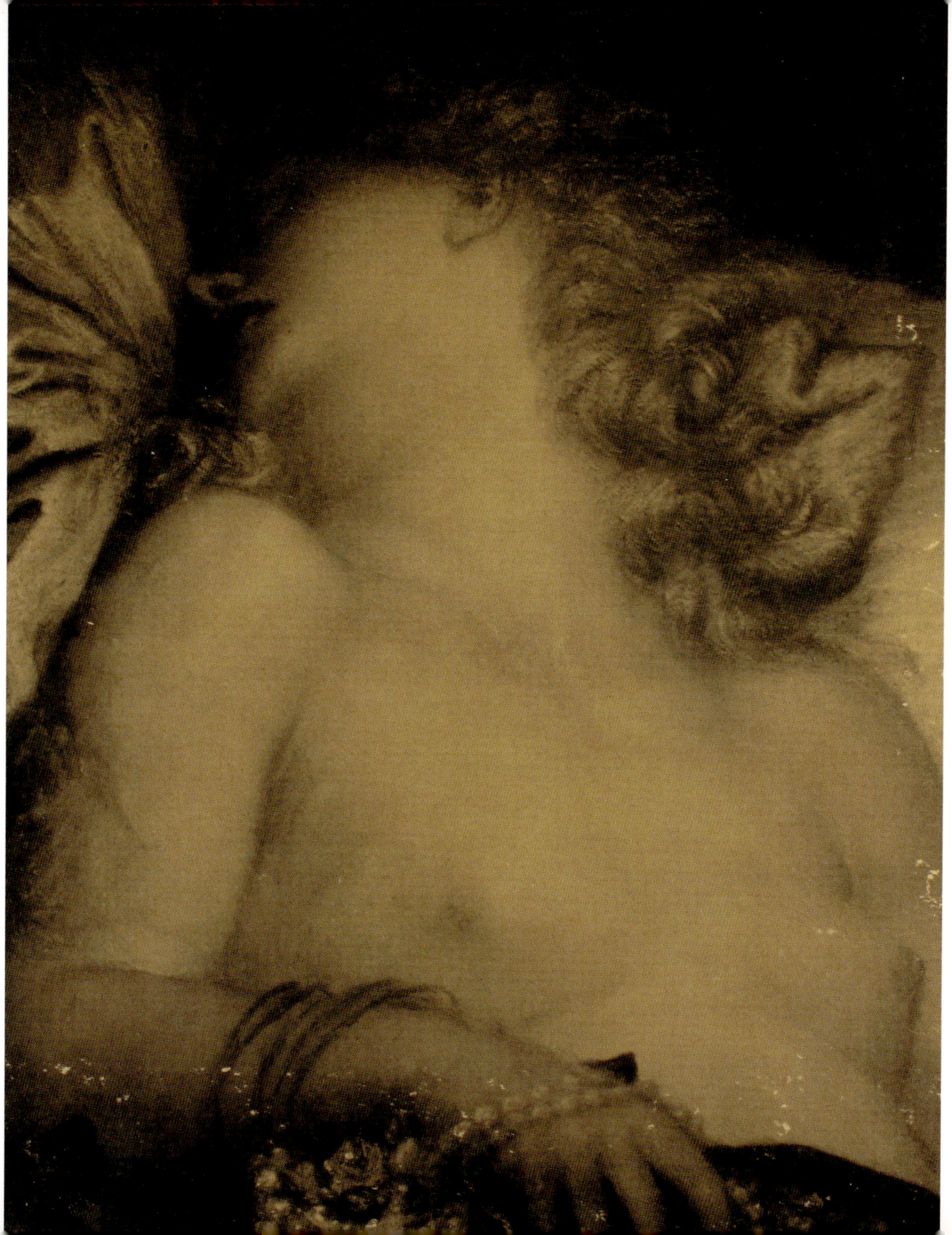

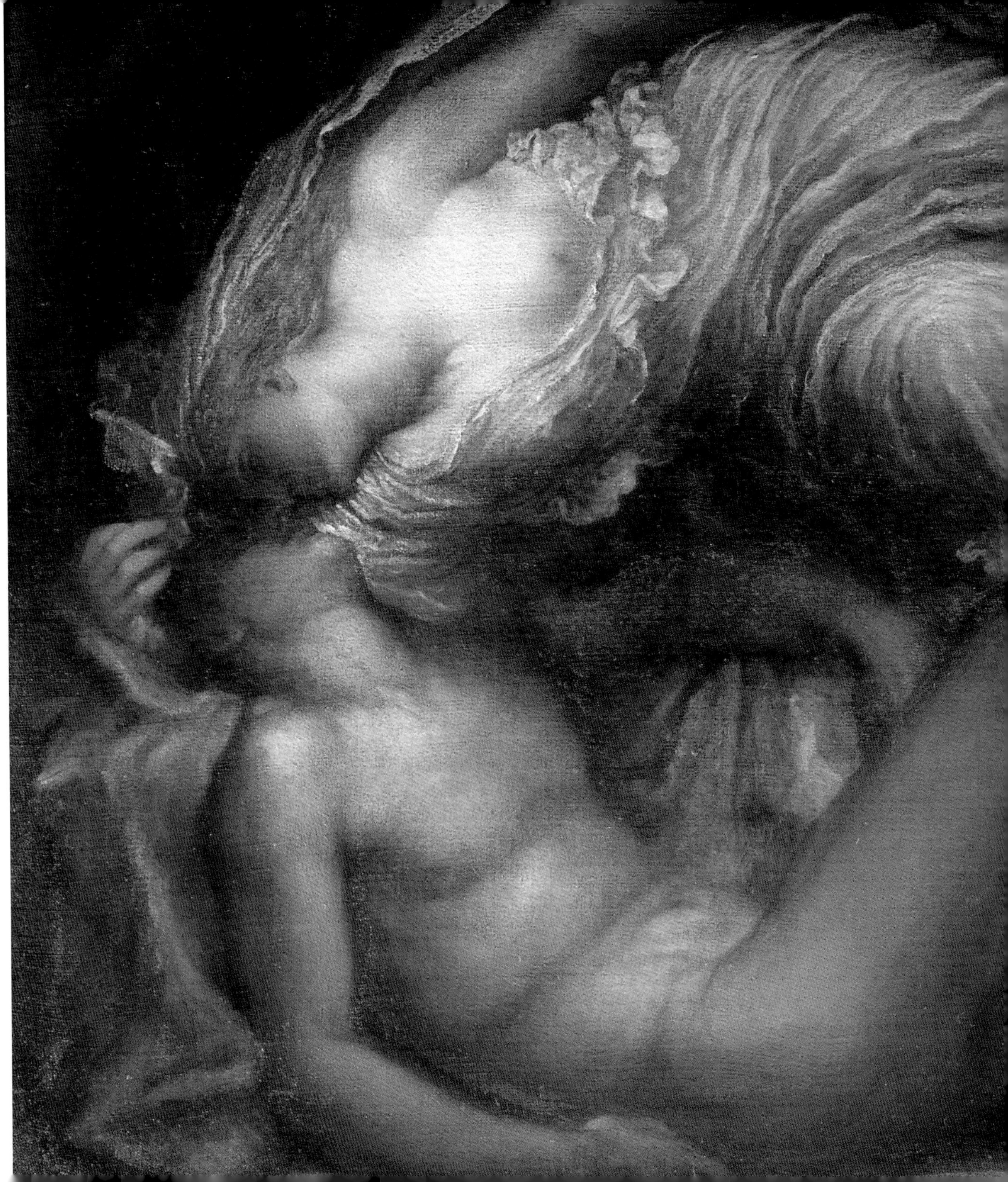

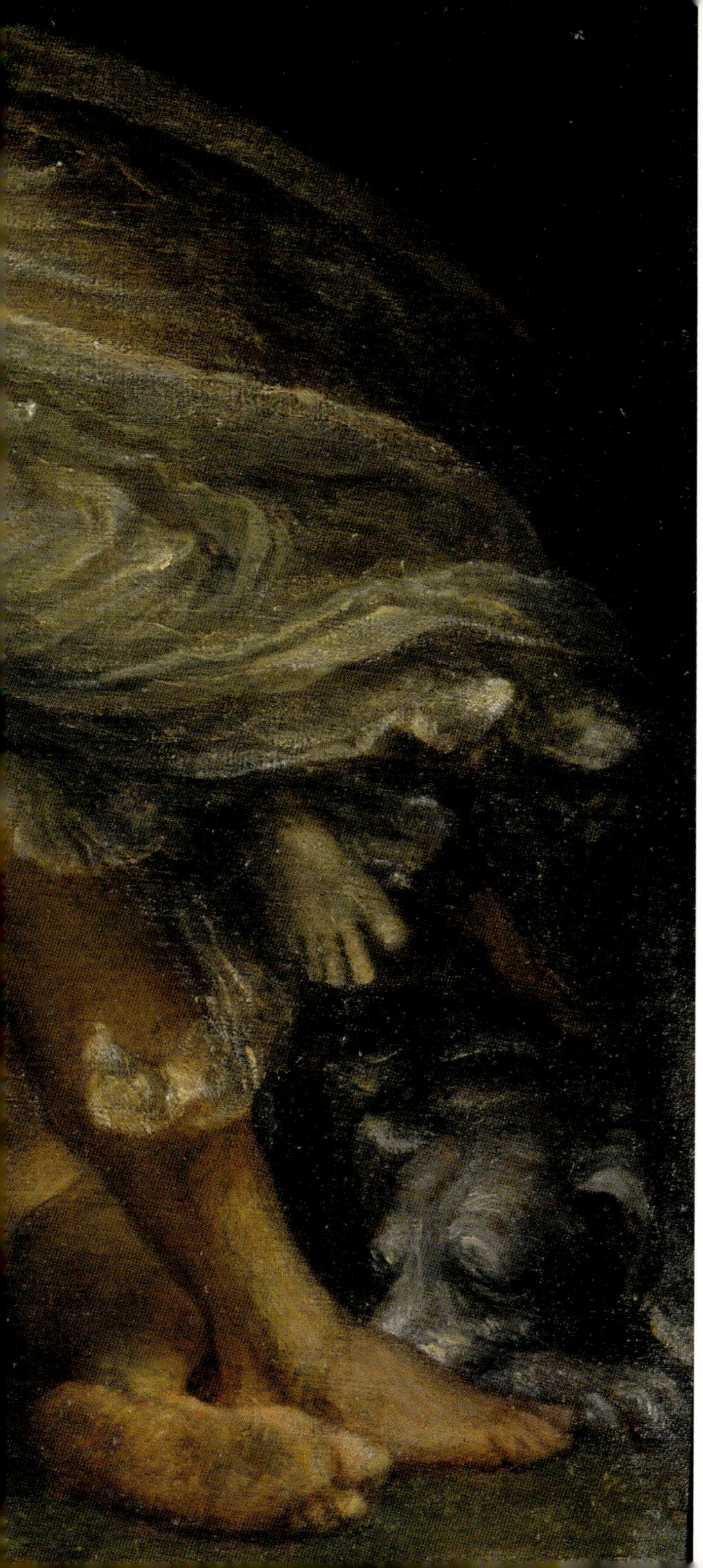

nymph spurned by Apollo twists back to face the sun-god and begins to metamorphose into a flower like a violet. 'Never was a divine legend translated into diviner likeness ... yearning with all the life of her lips and breasts after the receding light and the removing love – this is the Clytie indeed whom sculptors loved for her love of the Sun their God', marvelled the poet Algernon Swinburne. 'The splendour of her sorrow is divine.' Breaking away from the repose of classical sculpture, *Clytie* was hailed as the forerunner of the New Sculpture movement.[28]

Terry, dissatisfied after a brief return to the stage in Kate's shadow, vanished in October 1868. Sir Michael Holroyd relates that she had left in her room a photo of her husband's painting '*Found Drowned*' of a woman who had leaped to her death in the Thames. Hearing that her parents had had to identify a drowned woman, Terry flew home to reassure them before returning to live with Godwin, now a leading architect and art-furniture designer, in Hertfordshire.[29]

Meanwhile, her estranged husband's visionary painting of the moon goddess Diana swooping down to embrace the sleeping *Endymion* (Figure 23) who cannot wake to receive her love, reflects the artist and his moon goddess Terry. She is the inspiration for his key universal series on Eve, as the newly awakened woman and mother of mankind, symbolising the mind of modern times. (Major versions of these and

Opposite: (Figure 23) G F Watts, *Endymion*, 1869. Oil on canvas. Private Collection, image courtesy of Nevill Keating Pictures

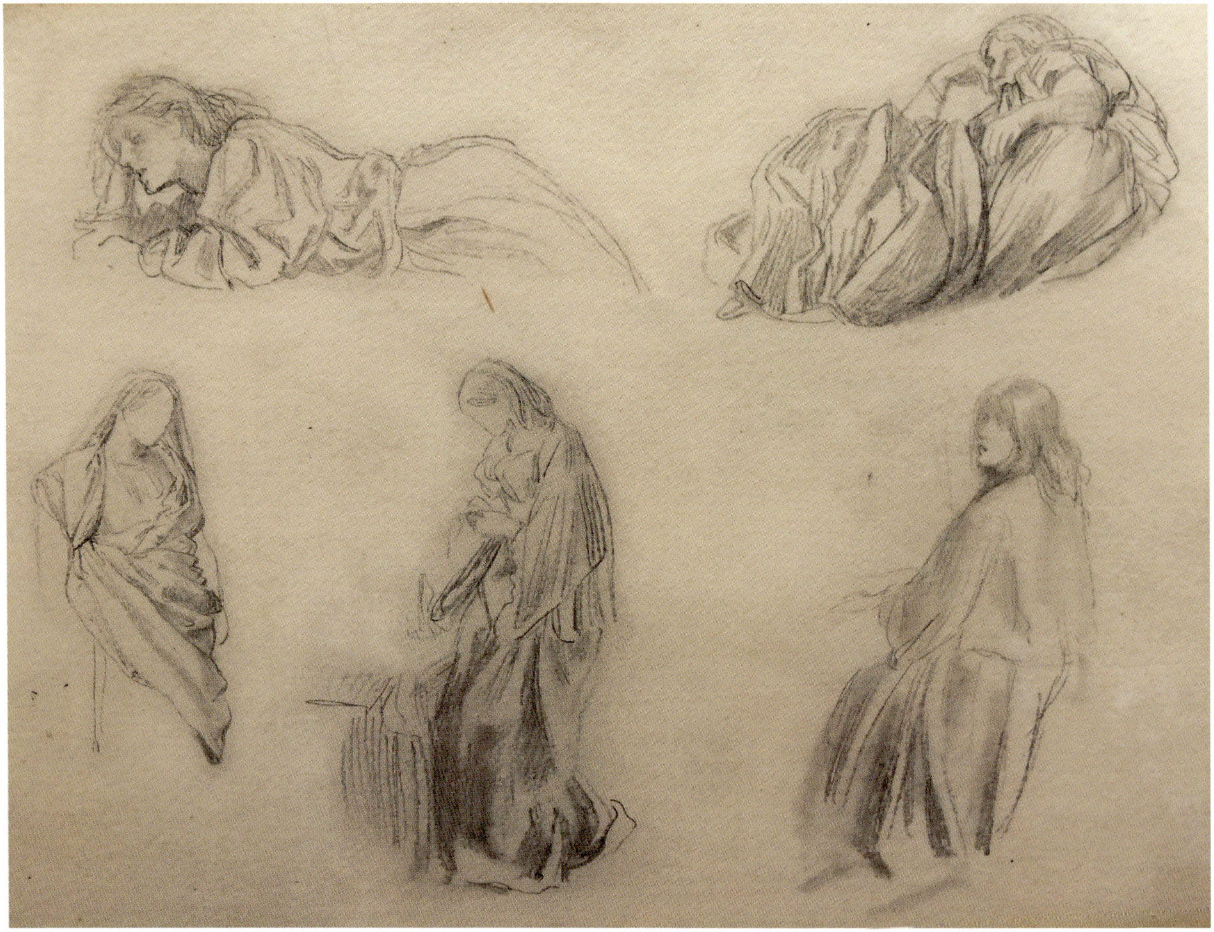

all others in this paragraph were given to the Tate in 1897.) In *She Shall be Called Woman*, or as the picture was first called, *Eve in the Glory of her Innocence*, she is seen as the central figure of the universe, newly created, emitting light. *Eve Tempted in the Garden of Eden* has the energy of Terry's portrait at the theatre curtain. The tender Angel of Death in *Time, Death and Judgement* was worked up from a drawing of his bride in delicately arranged robe (Figure 24).

Terry herself, having furthered her artistic education with Godwin, had made a triumphant return to the stage, notably in *The Merchant of Venice* in Squire Bancroft's company at the Prince of Wales Theatre. Her outstanding performance as *Olivia* at the Court Theatre, spurred Irving invited her to play Ophelia to his Hamlet, opening on 31 December 1878, inaugurating their 24-year partnership at the Lyceum Theatre. That year, within months of their divorce and her remarriage, Watts had developed his painting of Terry as *Ophelia* (Figure 20) into an idealised figure for exhibition at the Grosvenor Gallery in Bond Street where the Academician and actress were both stars – he as an exhibitor, she as the Aesthetic woman. This haunting symbolic painting shows how radically he thinned the face, hand and hair, eliminating the charm of his young wife to intensify the pathos and sense of foreboding. He enlivened her theatre photographs by Window and Grove into compelling life-size drawings. Her experience as Watts's wife surely informed Terry's own later international lectures on Ophelia:

> The whole tragedy of *her* life is that she is afraid ... Shakespeare's only timid heroine. She is scared of Hamlet when trouble changes him ... into a strange moody creature, careless of his appearance, bitter in his speech, scornful of society ... She is scared of life itself when things go wrong ... It is not surprising that she should think Hamlet mad, for all he says in the scene in which she returns his presents is completely beyond her. If this scene is rightly acted, we feel a great compassion for the poor girl, whom Hamlet at once loves and hates.[30]

Terry sat to a number of women artists, the first her friend Mary Ann Hall, followed by a prolific series of

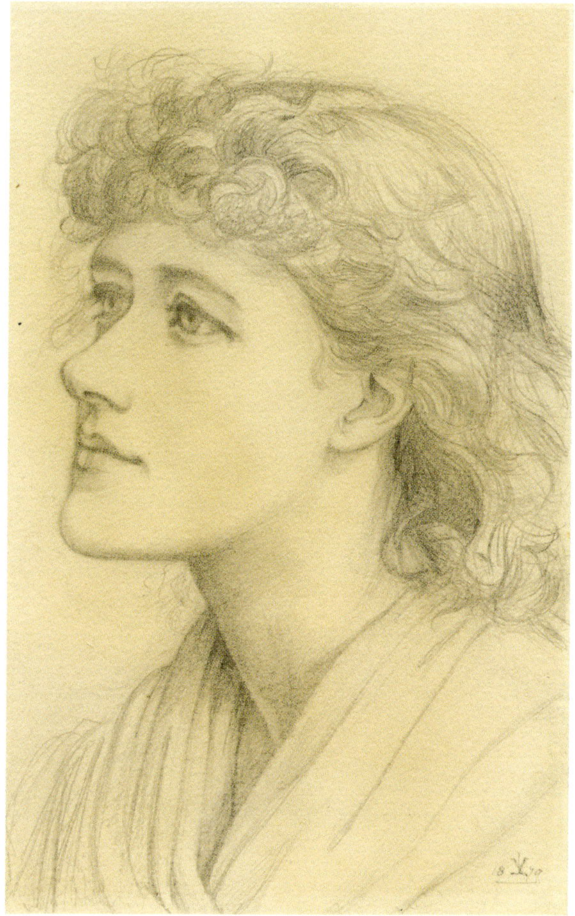

Opposite: (Figure 24) G F Watts, Sheet of studies of Ellen Terry, c.1864. Pencil on paper. Private Collection

Above: (Figure 25) Violet Lindsay, later Duchess of Rutland, *Ellen Terry*, 1879. Pencil on paper. Watts Gallery

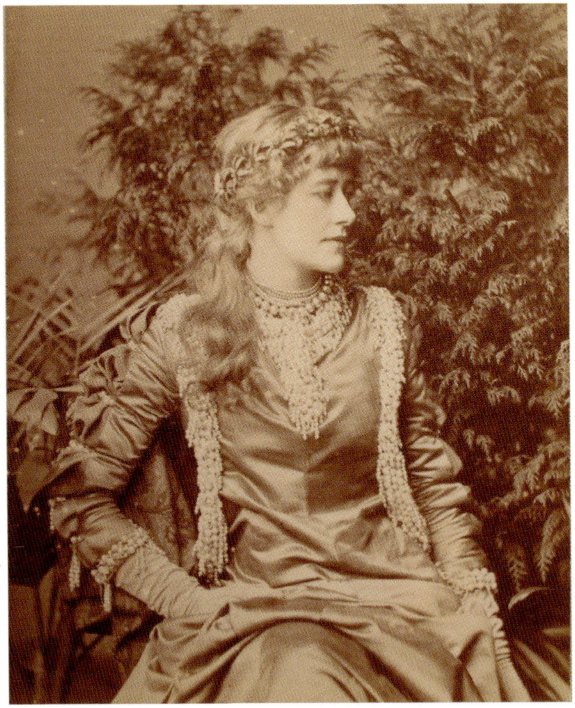

Above: (Figure 26) Window & Grove, *Miss Ellen Terry as 'Juliet'*, date unknown. Carte de visite. The Rob Dickins Collection, Watts Gallery

Opposite: (Figure 27) Anna Lea Merritt, *Ellen Terry as Ophelia*, 1880. Etching. National Portrait Gallery

drawings by Violet Lindsay (later Duchess of Rutland) (figure 25). Anna Lea Merritt, commissioned by *The Etcher* to represent Terry as Ophelia, captured her tearful face as the actress came off stage still in role (Figure 27). Louise Jopling, who in 1883 painted the fine portrait of Terry red-robed as Portia in *The Merchant of Venice* awaiting the verdict of the judge, achieved stillness in the restless actress by asking her to declaim 'Bid me tear the bond'. Irving bought the portrait and hung it in the famous Beefsteak Room at the Lyceum Theatre. Interestingly, rather than feature Terry herself, Sir John Everett Millais who painted Irving for the Garrick Club that year, instead borrowed the dress to transform his painting of another model into Portia (1886).[31] In Albert Moore's head of *Portia* (1885), he blends his softer featured model with Terry's hair and jaw.

Irving looked to Terry for guidance on colour, costume and lighting because 'I had learned from Mr Watts, from Mr Godwin, and from other artists, until a sense of decorative effect had become second nature to me'.[32] Her appearance as Portia in a golden dress at the Lyceum in 1879 sent the young Graham Robertson into raptures ('Her Portia ... is like a dream of beautiful pictures') and moved Oscar Wilde to compare her to a Venetian painting:

> For in that gorgeous dress of beaten gold
> Which is more golden than the golden sun
> No woman Veronese looked upon
> Was half so fair as thou whom I behold.

The enraptured Wilde penned three sonnets to Terry, the first earlier that year, celebrating her Aesthetic appearance as Queen Henrietta Maria in W. G. Wills's drama *Charles I*:

> She stands with eyes marred by the mists of pain,
> Like some wan lily overdrenched with rain:
> ...Bravely she tarrieth for her Lord the King,

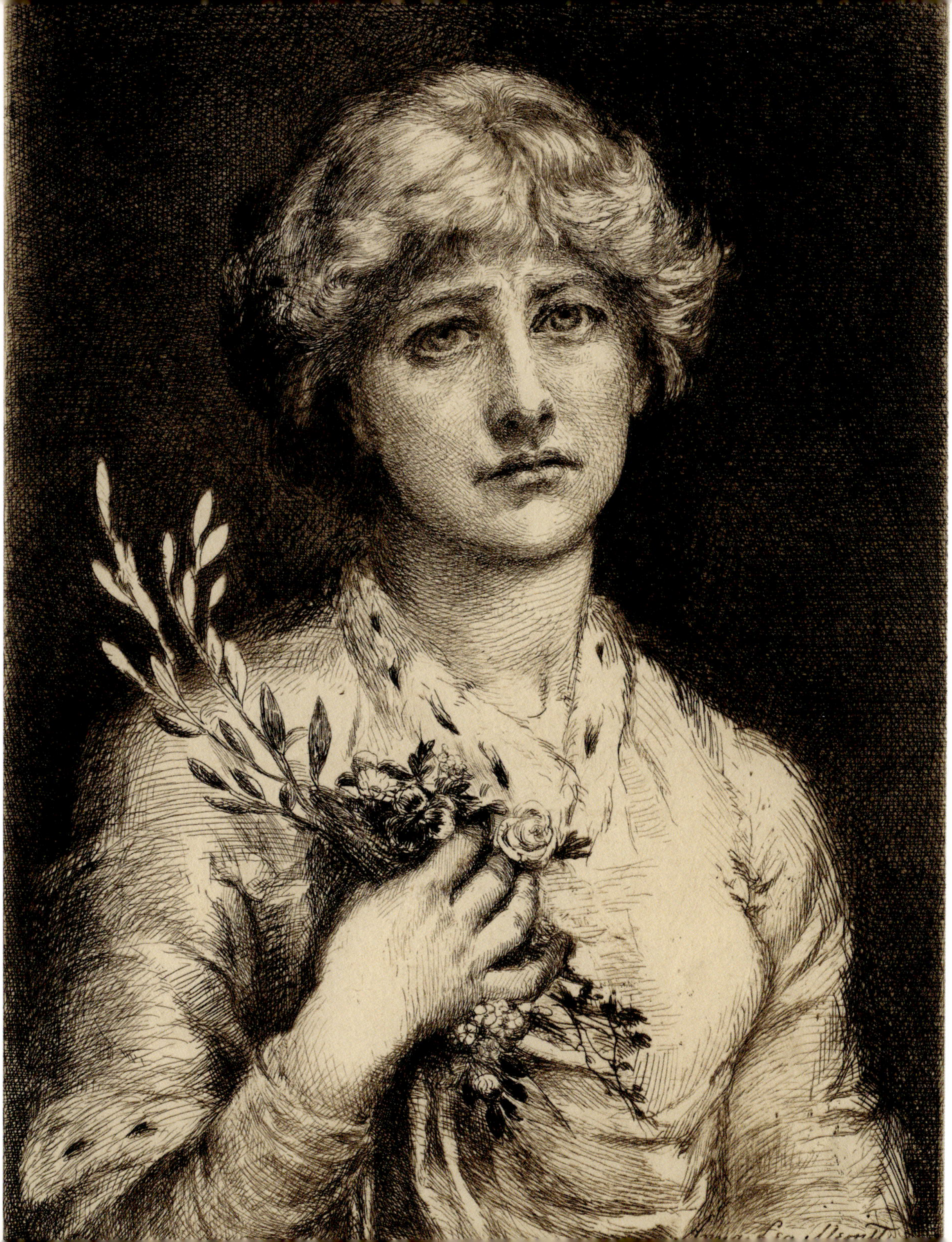

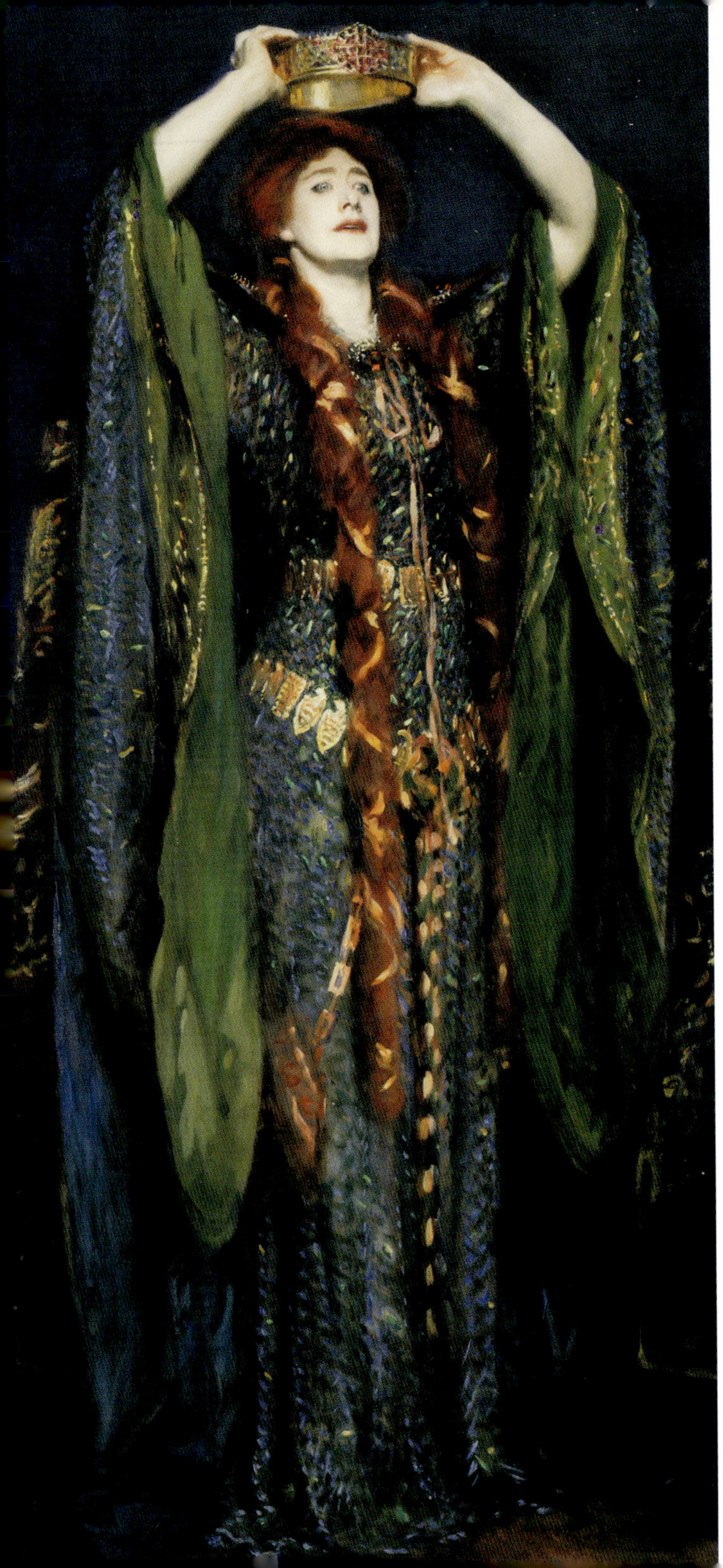

Her soul a-flame with passionate ecstasy.
O Hair of Gold! O Crimson Lips! O Face
Made for the luring and the love of man!

The Aesthetic vision of a 'wan lily', Terry felt, also conveyed her appearance as Ophelia. Performing Camma in *The Cup* in 1881, she inspired Wilde's third sonnet. This Tennyson play was, according to Terry, one of Irving's most beautiful productions. From the back of the vast Temple of Artemis, the many-breasted figure of Artemis loomed through a blue mist into yellow foreground lighting; and when the crowd raised their arms above their heads in a large, rhythmic, sweeping movement and bowed to the goddess, the effect was dynamic. Godwin had advised on the stage decoration, the ballet-effects and designed the silver three-handed cup and the toga Terry wore as Camma. To the drama critic William Archer, the temple scene was unprecedented, a masterpiece. This experiment would be developed by Terry and their son, Gordon Craig.[33]

Romeo and Juliet (1882), even more sumptuous and elaborate than *The Cup*, and performed before two prime ministers, William Gladstone and Benjamin Disraeli, was chosen for Terry, Irving said, to heighten the delight of their partnership. 'Every line suggests a picture. It is a dramatic poem rather than a drama.' But

Left: (Figure 28) John Singer Sargent, *Ellen Terry as Lady Macbeth*, 1889. Oil on canvas. Tate

Opposite: (Figure 29 & 30) Edward Burne-Jones, *Ellen Terry as Guinevere in Comyns Carr's King Arthur* (detail), 1894-5. Both charcoal over graphite underdrawing on Oriental paper. Smallhythe Place, National Trust

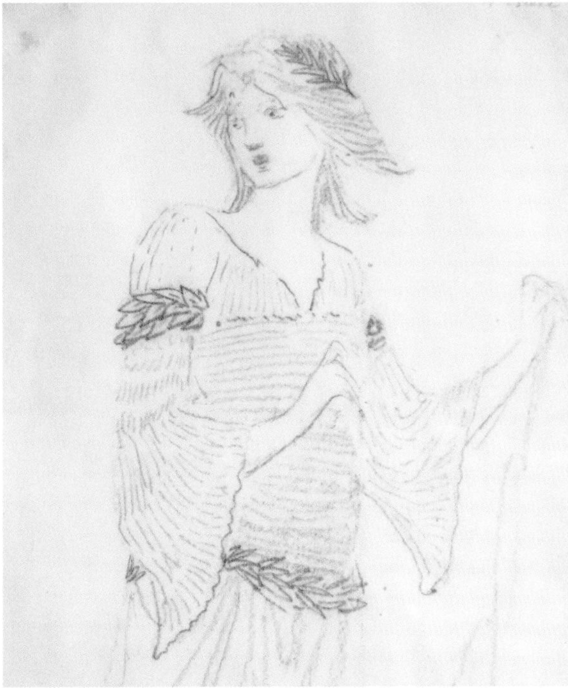

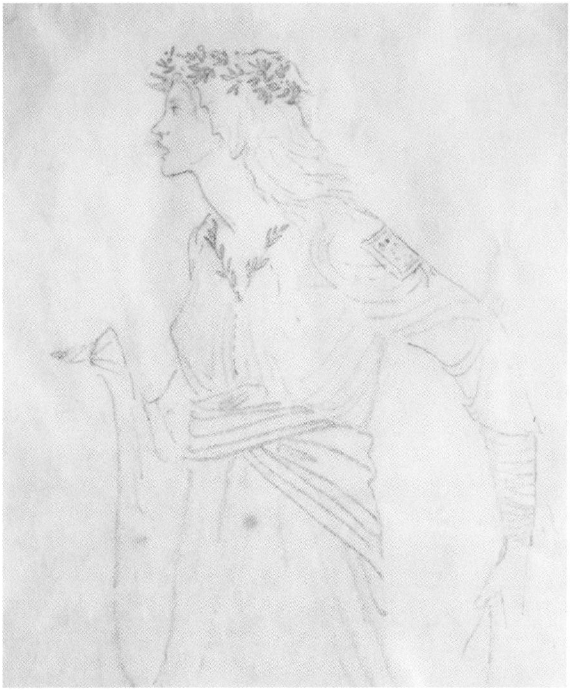

she felt she did not *look* right (Figure 26) and wished she had gone to Verona to imagine Juliet.[34] Beatrice in *Much Ado About Nothing* epitomised Terry's exuberance. She inscribed her theatre photographs in this role: 'There was a star danced, and under that I was born' (Figure 51). As Bram Stoker, Irving's business manager at the Lyceum and author of *Dracula*, put it, it was as though Shakespeare had a premonition of her coming: 'Surely never such a buoyant, winsome, merry, enchanting personality was ever seen on the stage – or off it.'[35]

That year, 1882, Watts happened to glimpse Terry through the hedge of his London garden and they began a loving, secret correspondence. 'Will you shake hands with me (in spirit?)', he asked. She answered simply, 'Yes'. He rejoiced in her success. His words making her dizzy 'with exquisite waves of feeling', he agreed to regard their marriage as a story both had read:

> As Artists we can still wander hand in hand through the images of the beautiful, & if it can be an encouragement to you & a help to you in striving after real greatness as distinct from mere success, to know that your efforts will be appreciated & honoured by me, do believe that no one has a more intense interest in them.

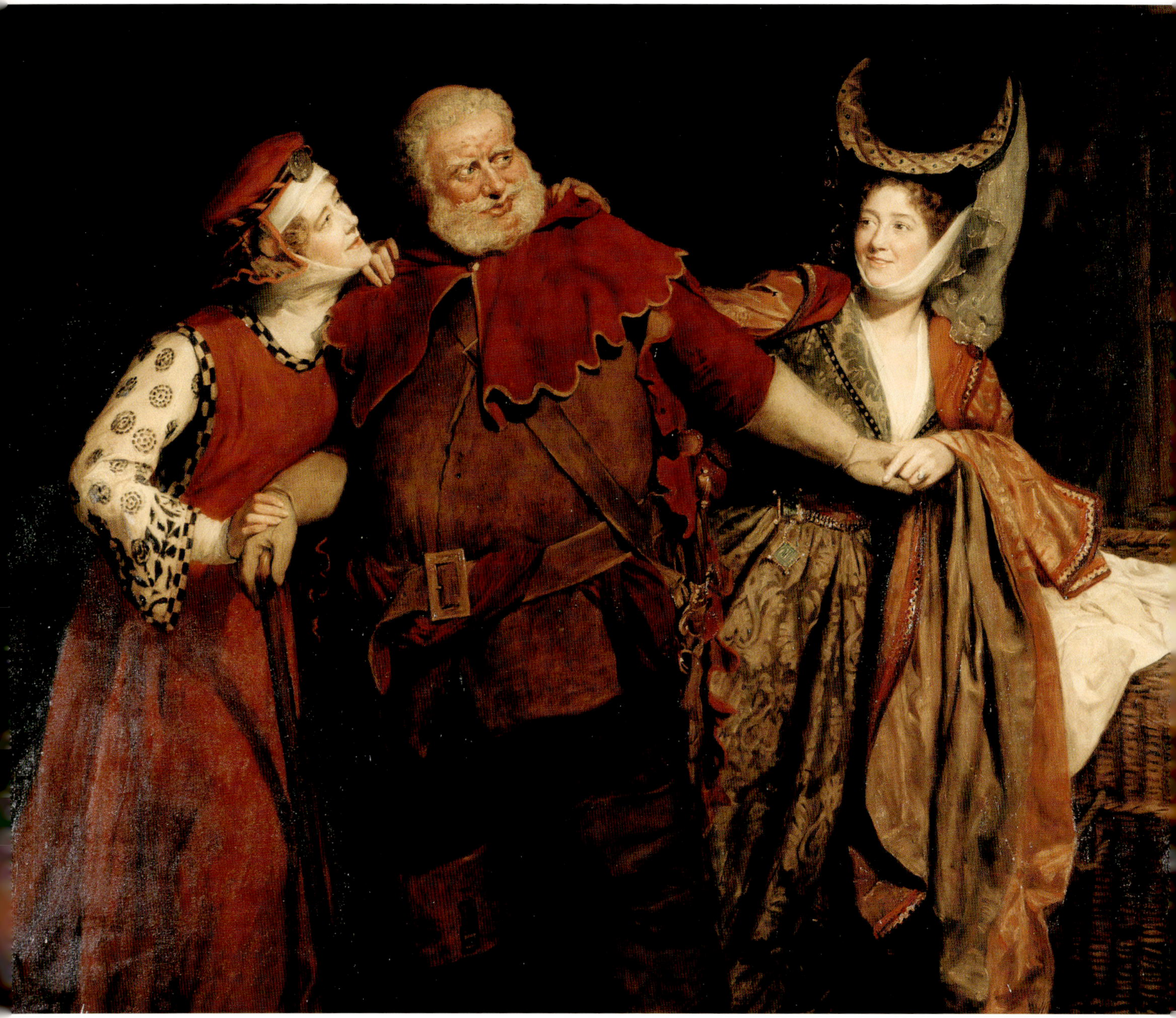

He sent her as a gift the theatre curtain portrait painted in 1864 (Figure 15). Delighted that 'your genius found its higher sphere & scope', he sent a 'phosphoric flicker of aspiration'. Watts's opalescent picture of the Scandinavian mythological spirit fairy *Uldra*, having Terry's youthful radiance, mesmerised critics at the Grosvenor Gallery and in America: 'the genius of the painter is prismatic, many coloured, sounding the depths of human thought, rising to the heights of human aspiration, and holding the experience of the ages in the hollow of its hand.'[36] This ethereal, poetic quality would be embraced by the European Symbolists.

On the first of a series of extremely successful Lyceum tours of America, in 1883, Terry captivated even the Attorney-General – 'What a creature, What a Queen! She smote me with the sword of her beauty, and arose her Knight!' Watts's retrospective exhibition, a landmark event soon to open at the Metropolitan Museum of Art in New York, intrigued the actress, who asked for the news report 'of our great painter, sculptor – I wish I could have made his sun shine'. Watts had photographs of all his pictures sent to her, touched by her response to *Hope* (1886), soon to cause a stir at the Grosvenor Gallery, as 'a picture of your own painting'.[37]

Macbeth (1888) marked a turning point in the history of the Lyceum, according to Terry. Her analysis of Shakespeare's character of Lady Macbeth and study of Albrecht Dürer's *Melancholia*, led her to reject Sarah Siddons's fiendish eighteenth-century performance in favour of a deeper, more womanly

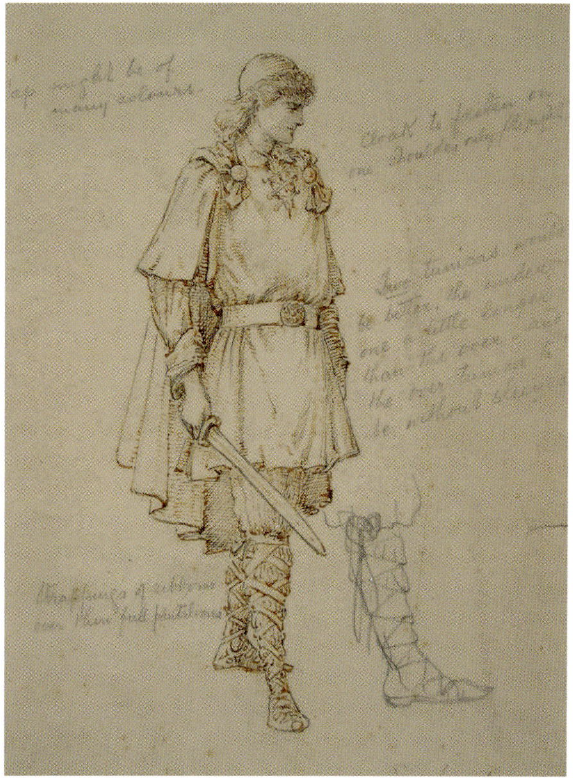

Opposite: (Figure 31) John Collier, *'The Merry Wives of Windsor' by William Shakespeare, with Herbert Beerbohm Tree as Falstaff, Ellen Terry as Mrs Page, Madge Kendal as Mrs Ford*, 1904. Oil on canvas. The Art Archive / Garrick Club

Above: (Figure 32) Lawrence Alma-Tadema, *Costume design for Dame Ellen Terry as Imogen in William Shakespeare's 'Cymbeline'*, 1896. Sepia ink and pencil on paper. Smallhythe Place, National Trust

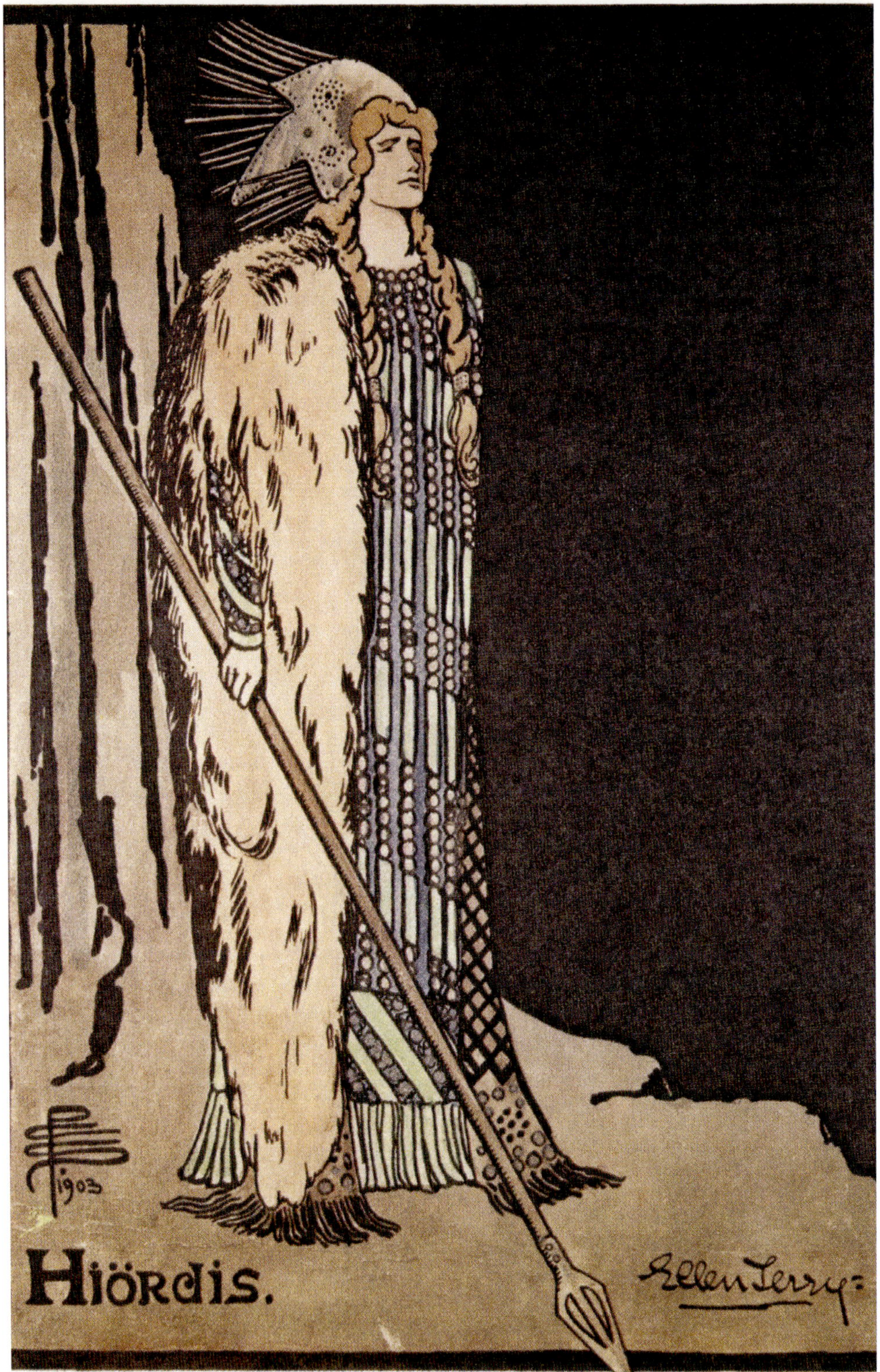
1903
Hiördis.
Ellen Terry

likeness. Burne-Jones, excited by her 'marvellously poetic harmony' of presence, voice and movement, found her beetle-wing dress 'grandly imagined and grandly worn'. Based on a medieval pattern by the French architect Eugène Viollet-le-Duc, the dress was designed by Alice Comyns Carr to shimmer like the scales of a serpent. 'The whole thing is Rossetti', Terry enthused, admiring the 'rich stained-glass effects'. Sargent's first sketch (Smallhythe Place, National Trust) shows her sweeping out of Macbeth's castle to welcome Duncan, the King of Scotland. To capture the exact swirl of her dress, Sargent made her walk up and down his Tite Street studio. 'That's it, that's it!' he exclaimed and rushed to the canvas. But it was the single regal figure of Terry as Lady Macbeth that he painted to completion, adjusting the colour as Burne-Jones recommended (Figure 28). Encapsulating, as the *Times* reported, 'the clash of two supreme emotions – of ambition, and of the sense of crime accomplished and the moral law thrown down'. The portrait characterises the actress rather than her role, suggests Richard Ormond, director of the John Singer Sargent catalogue raisonné and is 'a dazzling piece of Impressionist painting'. Much admired by Terry – 'Mr Sargent has idealized me, & of course I am delighted he has done so' – the picture was bought by Irving and hung in the Beefsteak Room at the Lyceum.[38]

While the actress transfixed her Chicago audience in 1893, Sargent's portrait of *Ellen Terry as Lady Macbeth* was on display there at the World's Fair (Figure 28). On show there too was Terry's teenage face and aspiration as the focus of Watts's *Love and Life* (Figure 19). Soon to be presented to found a national gallery of art in America, the picture represents 'Naked, bare Life sustained and helped up the steeps of human conditions, the path from the baser existence to the nobler region of thought and character'. This universal subject, Watts's most important message to the era, reflects Terry's frailty at Little Holland House and her gradual rise to fame.

George Bernard Shaw, with whom Terry engaged in a powerful epistolary courtship in the 1890s, declared Joseph Comyns Carr's drama *King Arthur* (1895) to be 'a splendid picture', more of a picture-opera than a play. Burne-Jones, then working on his vast painting of *Arthur in Avalon*, regarded the subject as his territory, sent drawings (Figure 29 & 30) and coloured sketches for Terry's costumes and the Byzantine hall of Camelot, the latter magnified by the Lyceum scene-painter Hawes Craven. Terry was however unhappy with her part as Guinevere (Figure 50), scribbling 'Dreadful' in her script. By contrast, as Imogen in *Cymbeline*, she gave an inspired performance. Terry was at first reluctant to wear the stunning costume designed for her by Alma-Tadema, which she thought might appear unbecomingly tight (Figure 32). But the Dutchman had his way and Terry's costume – 'one of the loveliest dresses I ever wore' as she eventually accepted (Figure 47) – set Aesthetic fashion *à la* Tadema at Liberty's.[39]

Opposite: (Figure 33) Pamela Colman Smith, *Ellen Terry as Hiördis in Ibsen's 'The Vikings'*, 1903. Print on paper. Smallhythe Place, National Trust

As her partnership with Irving at the Lyceum drew to a close, Terry appeared with Madge Kendal and Herbert Beerbohm Tree in a rollicking performance of *The Merry Wives of Windsor* at His Majesty's Theatre in 1902 (Figure 31). Her dress was designed by her daughter Edith Craig. Terry moved briefly into management at the Imperial Theatre to showcase the dynamic lighting and stripped stage effects created by her son Gordon Craig. Shaw having criticised Irving for not producing Ibsen, Terry staged Craig's *The Vikings at Helgeland*, a stunning, if blinding production, and performed the fierce warrior wife Hiördis (Figure 33) in strips of leather. [40]

Crowds lined the streets all night for Terry's Golden Jubilee at Drury Lane Theatre on 12 June 1906. The greatest actors and actresses of the age came - Eleanora Duse from Italy, Gabrielle Réjane from France, Benoît-Constant Coquelin, Enrico Caruso, Mrs Patrick Campbell, Lillie Langtry and Charles Wyndham. Irving having died the previous year, Tree played Benedick to Terry's Beatrice in a performance of one act of *Much Ado about Nothing*. Twenty-two members of the Terry family appeared on stage in celebration, and guests left with a souvenir scroll printed by William Nicholson, showing Terry in her many roles spanning half a century (Endpapers). In 1910-15 she gave lectures on Shakespeare's women, in America and Australia, and from 1917-22 experimented in silent films. In 1925 Terry was appointed Dame Grand Cross of the British Empire.[41] To the artist and collector Graham Robertson, to whom she sat for portraits over three decades (Figure 34), the last painted six years before her death on 12 July 1928, Terry was '*par excellence* the Painter's Actress and appealed to the eye before the ear; her gesture and pose were eloquence itself'.[42] The Sargent and Jopling portraits show her charisma on stage, but the artist who captured her energy as well as her youthful spirit on canvas, and who, like Godwin, played a decisive part in her artistic development, was Watts. Modelling for him influenced her artistic taste and helped her to refine her harmony of line in the studio and theatre. 'She added what she learned in the studio to what she had already learned on the stage so successfully', wrote Shaw, 'that when I first saw her in Hamlet, it was exactly as if the powers of a beautiful picture of Ophelia had been extended to speaking and singing.'[43] Much as Gordon Craig might wish to deny Watts's influence on his mother, his art was imbued with that rare visionary breadth that inspired Terry. Her months with Watts, their combined imaginative power and passion, triggered an extraordinary momentum in his art, yielding a greater legacy than has been realised. To Terry, 'the dear Signor ... from first to last has been a beautiful influence in my life.' Watts was different, '*wonderful* – his work to the very last being his best.' Her own ground-breaking realism had touched audiences as never before. 'Artist to her fingertips', as Stoker described her, Dame Ellen Terry was 'an actress of such incomparable excellence that in her art as in our memories she almost stands alone – great amongst the great. Ellen Terry is a great actress, the greatest of her time.'[44]

Opposite: (Figure 34) Walford Graham Robertson, *Ellen Terry*, 1922. Oil on canvas. National Portrait Gallery

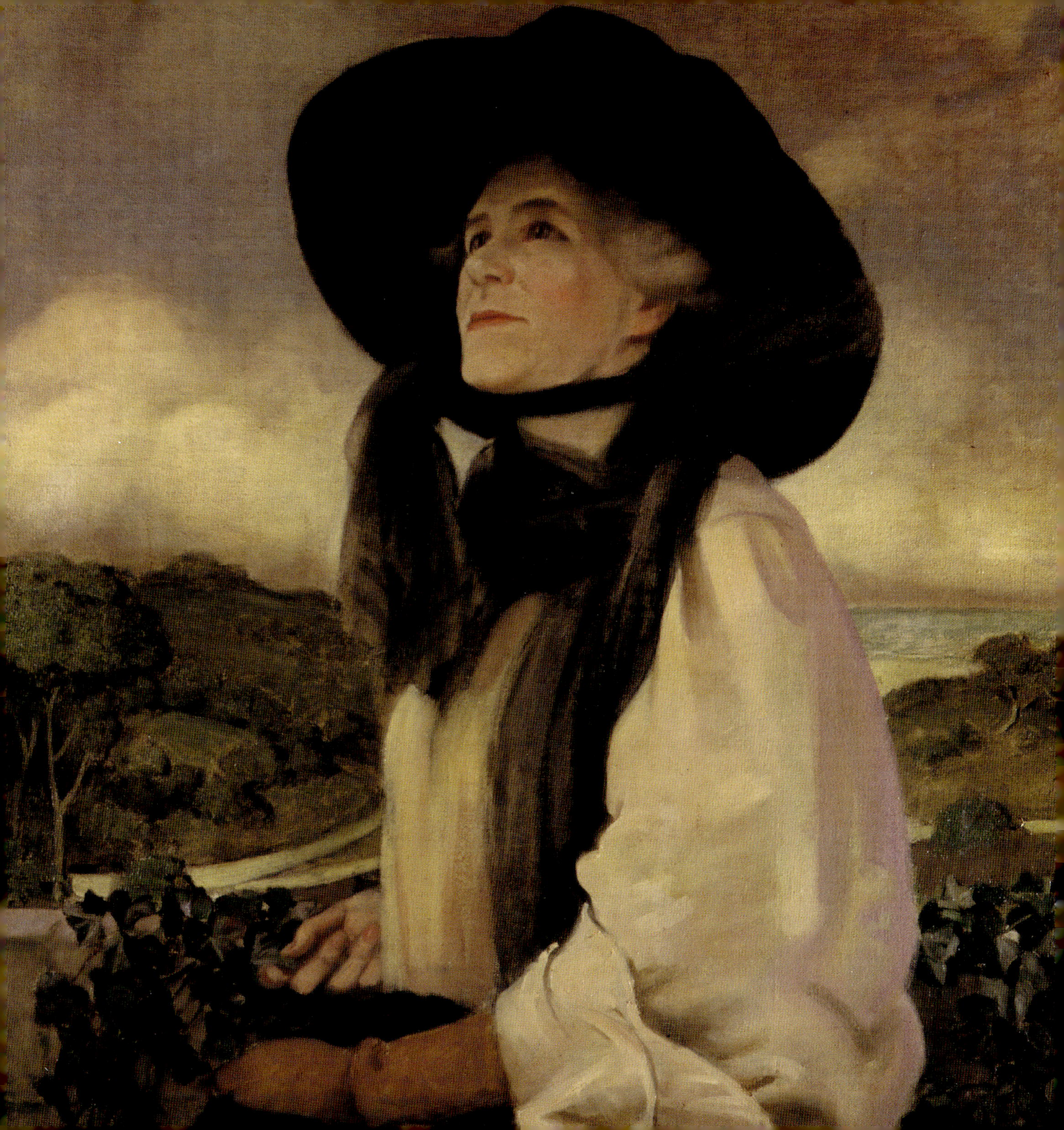

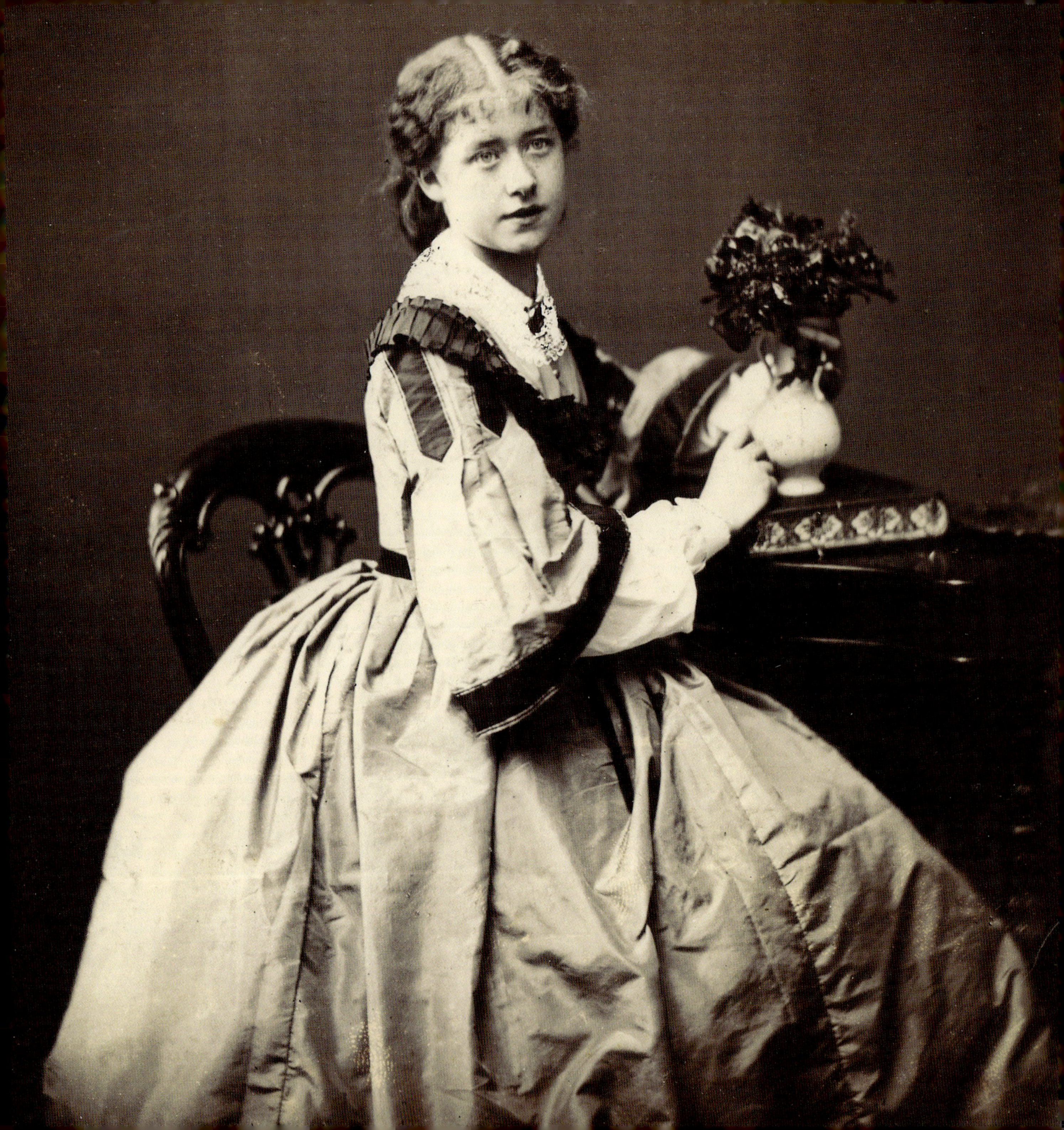

FASHIONING AESTHETICISM: ELLEN TERRY, PHOTOGRAPHY AND FASHION

Keremi Gawade

One of the most famous British actresses of her generation, Ellen Terry was also one of the most photographed women of the nineteenth century. An international touring performer, her fame extended well beyond the confines of the English stage. Throughout her career she posed for dozens of professional photographers, which in the words of theatre historian David Mayer allowed her to become a 'local, London (or capital city), national and international figure.'[45] As well as being immortalised in paintings by distinguished artists including George Frederic Watts and John Singer Sargent, Ellen Terry's photographic portraits are another important aspect of her iconography. The actress bequeathed to the public hundreds of photographic portraits, many of which can be found in public and private collections. Today these offer a unique insight into this *doyenne* of the Victorian and Edwardian stage, whilst also acting as a testament to Terry's artistic and aesthetic leanings, and her individual style. At the time, these portrait photographs were fundamental in promoting the actress and fuelled her celebrity. As we shall see, her photograph enjoyed immense currency in both Britain, where the *Shields Gazette Daily* reported in November 1894 that 'Miss Ellen Terry's photographs are in almost every window',[46] and abroad in America where she undertook extensive tours with Henry Irving and the Lyceum Company.

This essay focuses on the period 1875-1900 when Ellen Terry was at the height of her fame on both sides of the Atlantic. Specifically it will concentrate on the theatrical studio portraits that were produced in connection with her performances during this time, and cabinet cards that depict the actress in her own personal clothing. It will examine the confluence of woman, dress and photography, and how these merged to create a distinct fashionable discourse.

It is well recognised that Ellen Terry was sympathetic to the Aesthetic Movement, which had emerged in England in the mid-nineteenth century as a reaction to the industrialisation and materialism of the age. Extending to all aspects of living, the Aesthetic Movement came to embrace design, interior

Opposite: (Figure 35) Photographer unknown, *Ellen Terry aged 16*, 1864. Photograph. Smallhythe Place, National Trust

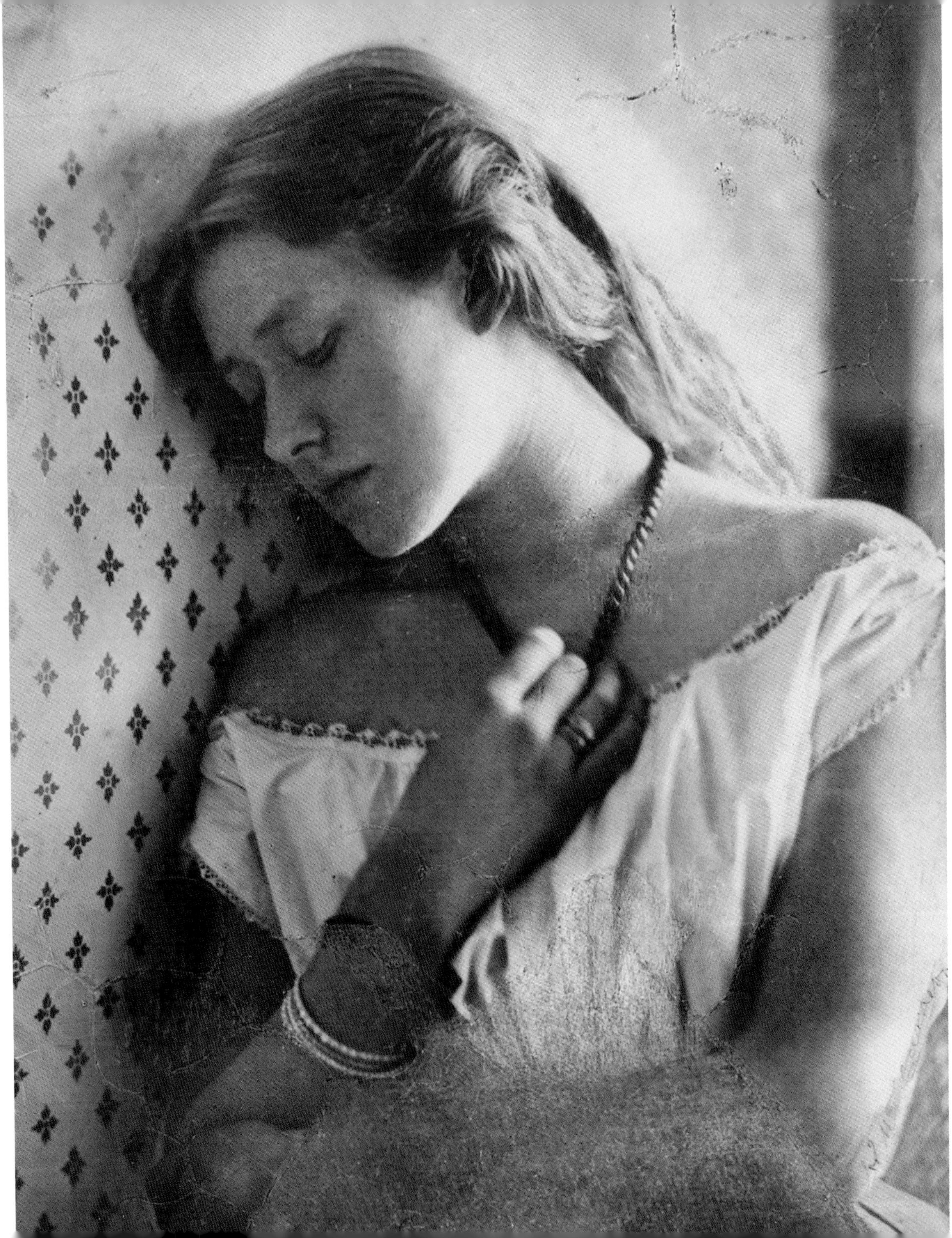

decoration, literature, architecture, photography and dress. The movement rallied to the call for 'Art for Art's Sake', championing 'an art self-consciously absorbed in itself, aware of the past but created for the present age, and existing only in order to be beautiful.'[47] As Terry herself has remarked in her memoirs, 'The aesthetic craze, with all its faults, was responsible for a great deal of true enthusiasm for anything beautiful.'[48] Dress became one of the most visible aspects of the Aesthetic Movement. Theirs was primarily an alternative style of dress, which rejected the rigid corsetry and cumbersome undergarments of mainstream fashion and instead denoted a preference for the beauty of the natural body, to be achieved through flowing form and fabric. Aesthetic dress also encouraged individuality and an eclectic approach to dressing, something for which Terry was celebrated and which can be discerned in her photographs. These offered a visual reference point for women in England and America wishing to emulate Aesthetic dress.

An early and celebrated photographic image of Ellen Terry is that taken by Julia Margaret Cameron in 1864 (Figure 36). Aged seventeen when it was taken, Terry had just left the stage to marry the considerably older G. F. Watts. Cameron captured the young bride on the Isle of Wight during the couple's honeymoon. Cameron herself was deeply immersed in the artistic, literary and intellectual circles of the mid-nineteenth century, allowing her to develop an unconventional and distinctive photographic style that owed much to the Pre-Raphaelite painters she was friendly with such as Dante Gabriel Rossetti and John Everett Millais. Often casting her sitters as tragic heroines, Terry is

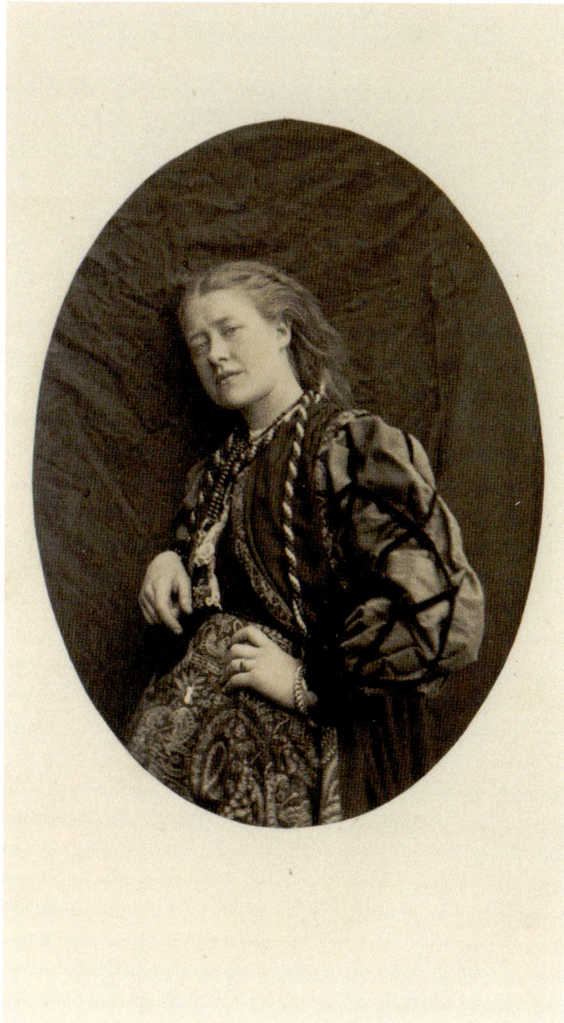

Opposite: (Figure 36) Julia Margaret Cameron, *Ellen Terry,* also known as *Sadness*, 1864. Photograph. Smallhythe Place, National Trust

Above: (Figure 37) Charles Dodgson (Lewis Carroll), *Mrs Watts*, 1865. Albumen Print. Gernsheim Collection, Harry Ransom Center, The University of Texas at Austin

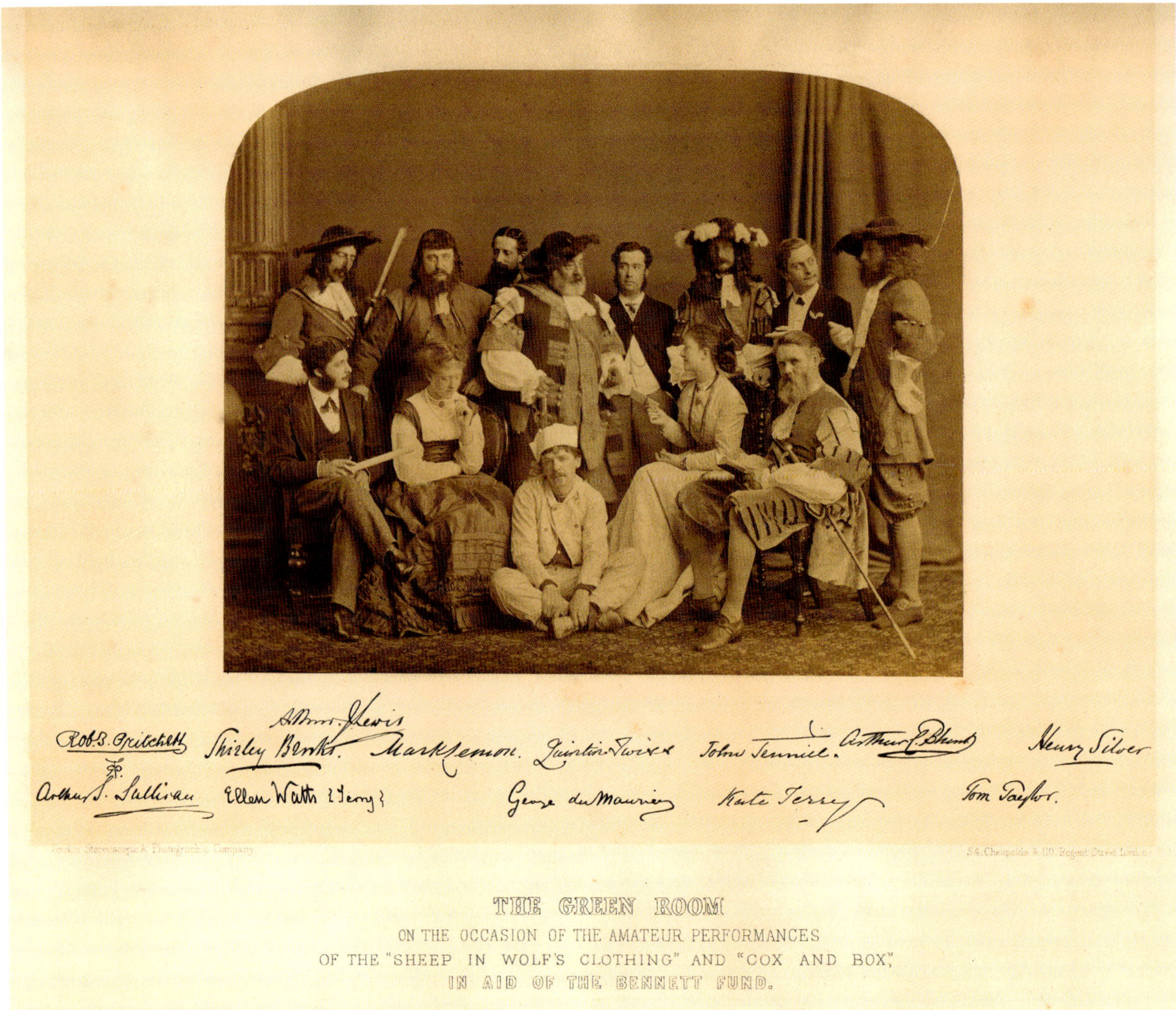

depicted as a child on the verge of womanhood and tinged with woeful sadness. The photograph also celebrates her pre-Raphaelite beauty, which was to captivate artists, intellectuals and the public alike for years to come. The critic Clement Scott said of Terry around this time that 'she was a young girl of enchanting loveliness. She was the ideal of every pre-Raphaelite painter, and had hair, as De Musset says, *comme le blé*.'[49] Compared to other photographic portraits of the period in which subjects were often placed within the formal, rigid confines of the studio, Cameron's image of Terry is unconventional, particularly from the point of view of its informality and her use of the 'close up' which creates a sense of intimacy. Along with Watts's famous portrait of Terry entitled *Choosing* (Figure 17), it is also an image that was important in creating a new identity for Terry as the quintessential pre-Raphaelite woman, an identity she was to be associated with throughout her adult life. In the 1880s, upon seeing the actress for the first time, the *New York Tribune* succinctly summed up the appeal of Terry to its readers: 'The face itself is a peculiar one. Though not by ordinary canons beautiful, it is nevertheless one to be remembered, and seems to have been modeled on that of some pre-Raphaelitish saint – an effect heightened by the aureole of soft golden hair escaping from under the plain brown straw and brown velvet hat.'[50]

Other early photographic portraits, such as those by Lewis Carroll, were equally important in positioning Terry in this artistic vein. In one photograph taken by Carroll she is wearing the wedding dress designed for her by William Holman Hunt, a brown silk gown worn without stays that evokes a strong medieval influence with its loose puffed sleeves and natural shape (Figure 37). Although by the date of this photograph Terry and Watts had separated, the groundwork had been laid and her artistic eye had been awakened and developed. The experience of being photographed by such figures in these artistic surroundings would certainly have a lasting influence on the young Ellen Terry. As the actress was later to write in her memoirs when discussing her artistic contribution to Lyceum productions:

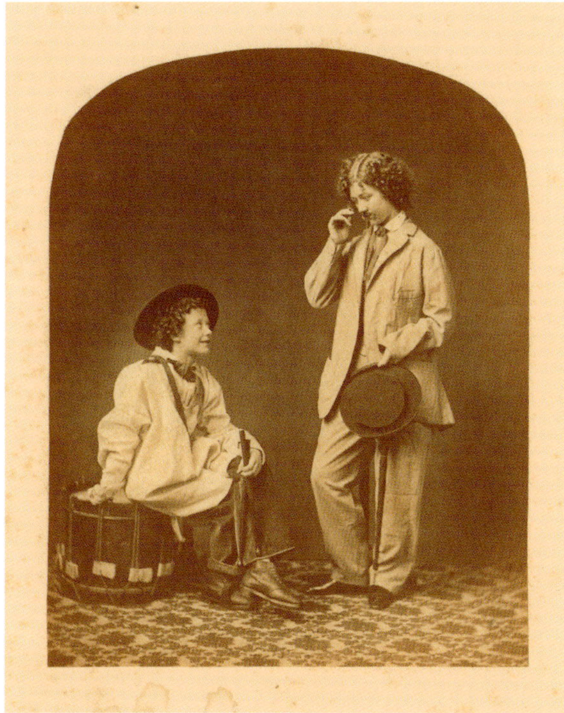

Opposite: (Figure 38) London Stereoscopic & Photographic Company, *The Green Room*, 11th May 1867. Albumen print. National Portrait Gallery

Above: (Figure 57) W.G. Lacy, *Dame Ellen Terry and Kate Terry in 'Distant Relations' a Drawing Room Entertainment*, c.1859. Photograph. Smallhythe Place, National Trust

'I brought help, too, in pictorial matters. Henry Irving had had little training in such matters – I had had a great deal. Judgment about colours, clothes, and lighting must be trained. I had learned from Mr. Watts, from Mr. Godwin, and from other artists, until a sense of decorative effect had become second nature to

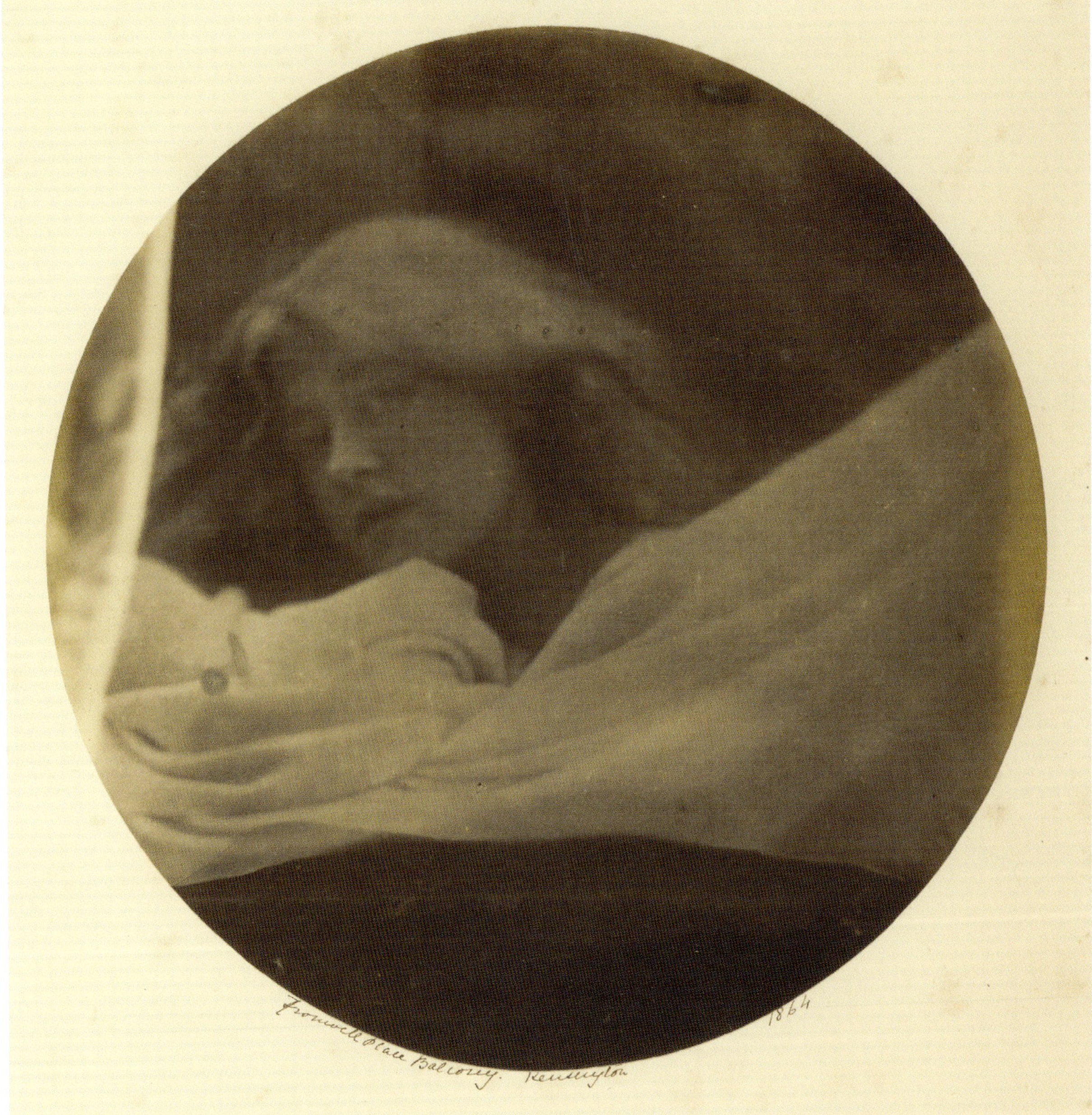
Cromwell Place Balcony. Kensington
1864

me.'[51] Such a close association with these cultural and artistic movements from an early age ensured that Ellen Terry was also able to foster a particular and unique image for herself as an actress, one that owed much to Pre-Raphaelitism and Aestheticism.

Born in 1847, Ellen Terry's early career coincided with the birth and rapid rise of photography. The actress was first photographed in 1856 when she appeared as Mamillius in Charles Kean's production of *The Winter's Tale*. This photograph, a salted paper print taken by Martin Laroche, is an early example of the type of theatrical portrait photography that was to become so popular during the second half of the nineteenth century (Figure 6). The image is significant as not only does it document Ellen's stage debut but also demonstrates early photographic techniques. In 1839 Louis Daguerre announced the first successful photography process, which consisted of a photographic image with a mirror-like surface that was made on a silvered copper plate. Named daguerreotypes, each image was unique, delicate and often protected by glass in a decorative frame. However, whilst revolutionary, producing daguerreotypes was a slow, laborious and expensive procedure. Daguerre's experiments and findings were made public, thus allowing for further developments in photography. The next important discovery was made by William Henry Fox Talbot, a British inventor and photography pioneer from Wiltshire. In 1841 Fox Talbot introduced a new photographic method called the calotype, which produced pictures on paper coated with silver iodide and which allowed for dozens of positive prints to be produced from a single calotype negative. Frederic Scott Archer further refined photographic practice with his invention of the wet-collodion process in 1851. This process produced a negative image on a glass plate and combined the benefits of both the daguerreotype and the calotype in that it produced a clear, sharp image akin to the daguerreotype, but also allowed for the reproduction of an unlimited number of prints from a single negative. These were usually albumen or salt prints.

Opposite: (Figure 39) Julia Margaret Cameron, *The South West Wind*, 1864. Albumen silver print. The J. Paul Getty Museum, Los Angeles

By the 1850s and coinciding with the beginning of Terry's acting career, significant technical advances had been made to democratise portrait photography and to make it available for public consumption. The great breakthrough came with André-Adolphe Disdéri's promotion of the *carte de visite* which he patented in 1854. The *carte de visite*, so named because it measured the same as a pocket-sized visiting card, was a by-product of the collodion process and used a multi-lens camera that could create multiple images on one plate. This not only cut costs, reducing the retail price of an image, but also allowed for larger quantities to be mass-produced. The result was the phenomenon aptly named *cartomania* that swept across Europe and America in the 1850s and 1860s. In Britain the royal family played a vital role in popularising the *carte de visite*. In 1860 J. E. Mayall took a series of photographs of Queen Victoria and her family that were published with great success as *cartes de visite* in 1861. The Queen's personal enthusiasm for this

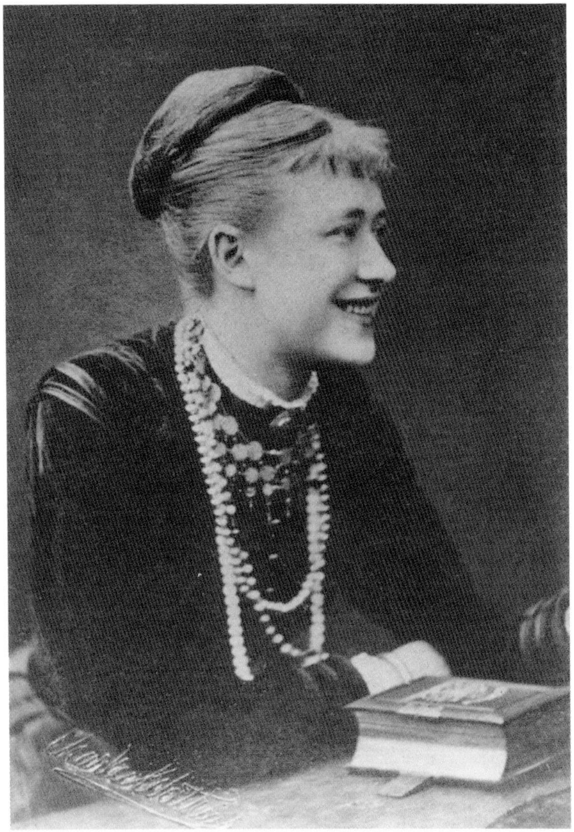

Above: (Figure 40) Herbert Watkins, *Ellen Terry*, c. 1872. Carte de visite. Smallhythe Place, National Trust

Opposite: (Figure (41) Napoleon Sarony, *Ellen Terry*, 1879. Cabinet photograph. Smallhythe Place, National Trust

new format helped to legitimise portrait photography and assured its acceptance by a middle-class public. Indeed, the *carte de visite* is recognised as one of the major forces in accelerating celebrity culture. Its small size made the *carte* easy to disseminate and for the first time images of famous personalities were readily available for the public to admire. As John Plunkett has observed, 'collecting *cartes* became the latest social fashion ... integrating public figures into the intimate arena of individual subjectivity.'[52] The early photographic portraits of Terry include a *carte de visite* series taken by Herbert Watkins (Figure 40). These studio portraits, dating from around 1872, depict the actress wearing a dark coloured velvet dress, distinctly Pre-Raphaelite in style, and multiple strands of beads. An eminent portrait photographer who opened his first photographic studio on Regent Street in the mid-1850s, Watkins photographed many luminaries of the day including Charles Dickens. His *carte de visite* portraits were readily available and highly sought after, as evidenced by an article in the *London Daily News* dating from 1858 that heaped praise on the photographer's work: 'The tiny bust portraits which he executes for the "calling cards" ... combine high artistic feeling with delicate finish. Many of them are not unworthy to rank, as works of art, with the engraved gems of the ancients.'[53]

The popularity of the *carte de visite* lasted until the mid-1860s, when it was superseded by the larger-format cabinet card, first introduced to Britain in 1866 by the photographic firm Window and Bridge in response to a slowing down of trade. The cabinet photograph addressed the need for a new product to captivate the public and consolidated the commercialisation of celebrity photography. The cabinet card was normally an albumen print produced from a wet-plate collodion negative and mounted on a card measuring 6½ by 4¼ inches. Cabinet cards featured a deep border at the bottom, allowing for text to be printed giving information on the sitter. This new format soon became the international standard and its popularity endured until the early twentieth century. Both the *carte de visite* and the cabinet card were avidly traded, collected and assembled into albums. As the cabinet card was also larger in scale than the *carte de visite*, it offered photographers more choice in terms of compositional arrangements. In addition to photographs of royalty, literary and artistic figures and politicians, there was a particularly high demand for photographs of actors and actresses. Indeed, Terry's career also coincided with the rise of the theatre as a respectable form of entertainment: from the 1840s Queen Victoria renewed royal support of the theatre, which boosted its moral and social standing both in England and America.[54] An insightful article which appeared in the *Observer* in 1879 discusses the popularity of amassing celebrity photographs and cites Ellen Terry as one of the most collectible personalities:

> It can hardly be called a morbid curiosity that tempts us to fill the conventional photograph album with representations of the Queen, the Prince and Princess of Wales, Mr. Ruskin, Mr. Millais, Mr. Irving, the Earl of Beaconsfield, Mr. Gladstone, Mr. Tennyson, Madame Patti, Miss Ellen Terry, and Mr. Spurgeon.[55]

As the theatre expanded and its reputation improved, there was a growing and insatiable demand for images of the most illustrious stars of the stage, and particularly actresses. A woodburytype photograph published in 1875 depicts a montage of photographic

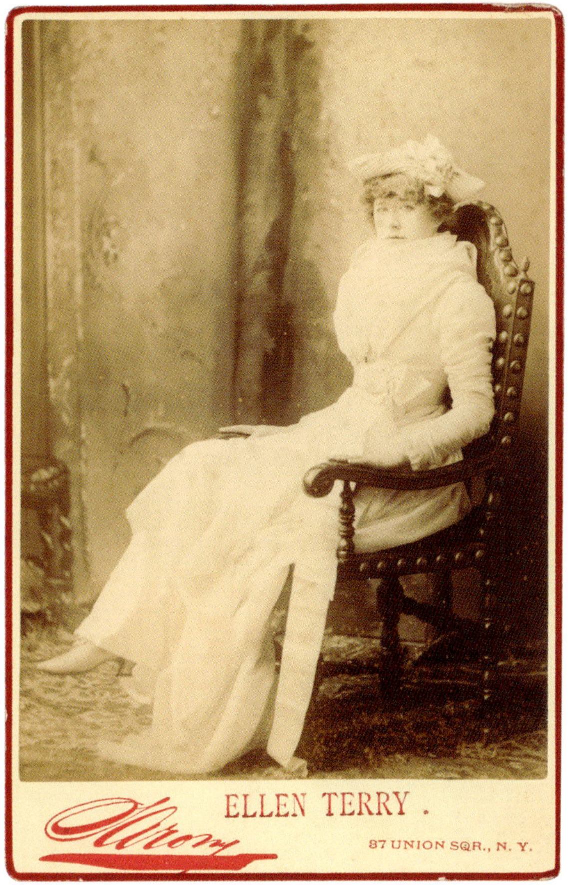

portraits of celebrated ladies of the London stage (including Ellen Terry), attesting to the immense popularity of the actress and her photographic image (Figure 42). Roger Hargreaves and Peter Hamilton note in their comprehensive study of nineteenth-century portrait photography how theatre and photography were a 'potent commercial mix' with the

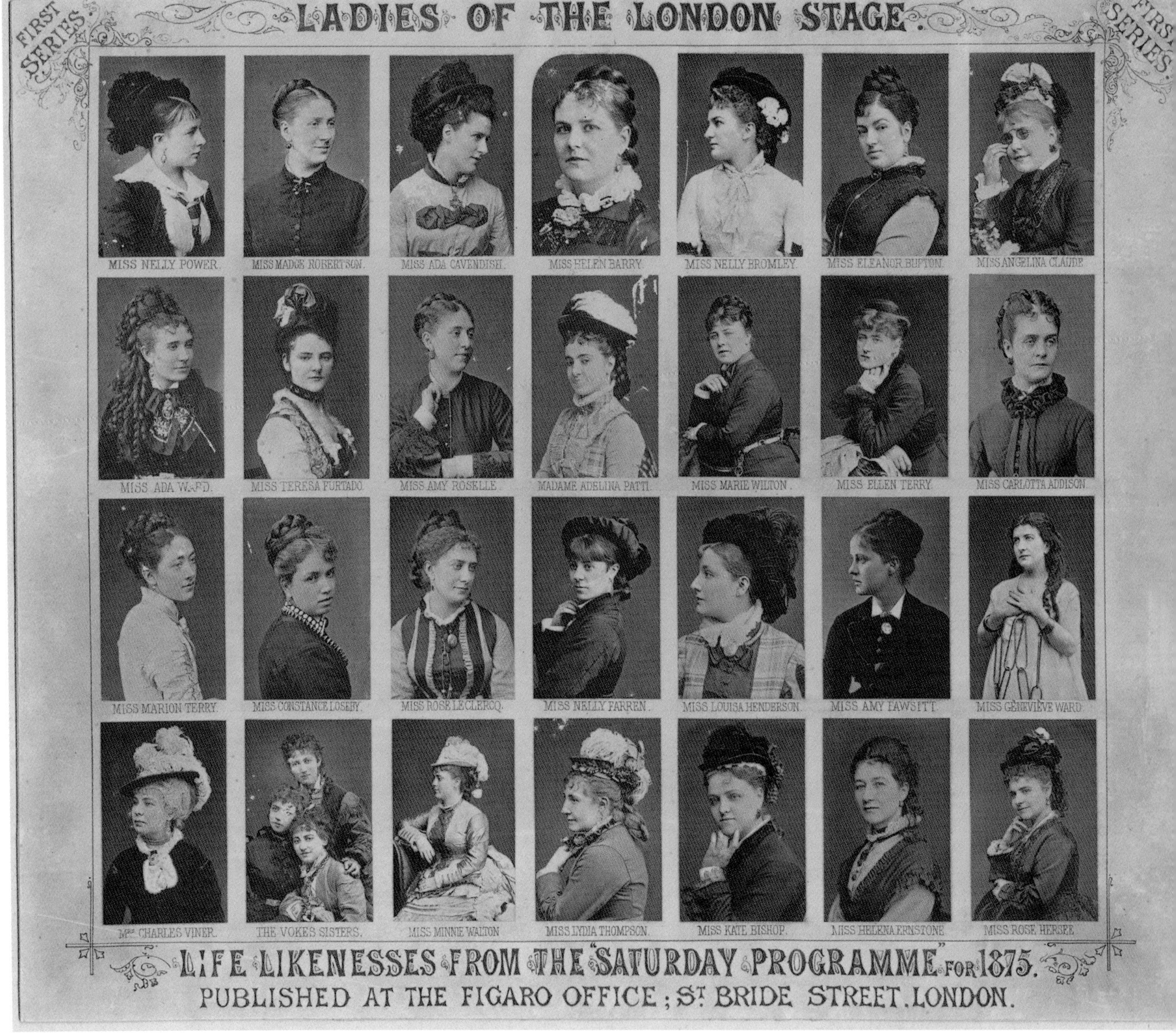
FIRST SERIES.
LADIES OF THE LONDON STAGE.
FIRST SERIES.
MISS NELLY POWER.
MISS MADGE ROBERTSON.
MISS ADA CAVENDISH.
MISS HELEN BARRY.
MISS NELLY BROMLEY.
MISS ELEANOR BUFTON.
MISS ANGELINA CLAUDE.
MISS ADA WARD.
MISS TERESA FURTADO.
MISS AMY ROSELLE.
MADAME ADELINA PATTI.
MISS MARIE WILTON.
MISS ELLEN TERRY.
MISS CARLOTTA ADDISON.
MISS MARION TERRY.
MISS CONSTANCE LOSEBY.
MISS ROSE LE CLERCQ.
MISS NELLY FARREN.
MISS LOUISA HENDERSON.
MISS AMY FAWSITT.
MISS GENEVIÈVE WARD.
MRS. CHARLES VINER.
THE VOKES SISTERS.
MISS MINNIE WALTON.
MISS LYDIA THOMPSON.
MISS KATE BISHOP.
MISS HELENA ERNSTONE.
MISS ROSE HERSEE.
LIFE LIKENESSES FROM THE "SATURDAY PROGRAMME" FOR 1875.
PUBLISHED AT THE FIGARO OFFICE; ST. BRIDE STREET. LONDON.

camera casting 'theatrical types in the new role of widely collected celebrities.'[56] The relationship was mutually beneficial. Photographers were eager to capitalise on the fame of a performer whose presence would bestow prestige on their photographic studio, thus encouraging further patronage, whilst the actor or actress would use photography to enhance their celebrity and further their career. Not only would photographs of celebrated stage personalities be sold in shops, news-stands and at the theatres, their portraits were also conspicuously displayed in the windows of photographic studios in populated city centres. Again Hargreaves and Hamilton remark upon the importance this was to have in fostering the new celebrity culture: 'This blend of shopping and celebrity viewing must have been something akin to an open-air version of flipping idly through a modern glossy magazine.'[57] The phenomenon of admiring celebrity photographic portraits in shop windows and collecting them was noted by the *Belfast Newsletter* in December 1885:

> Few passions, apparently, are so prevalent and so powerful as that for studying and, if possible, possessing the portraits of more or less distinguished people. The shop windows round which there gather the largest crowds are often those which exhibit to the view photographs or engravings, or the like, of the best-known men and women of the time.[58]

An actress of Ellen Terry's calibre and status would frequent the best photographic studios of the day. Each role required a new portrait, which would be widely disseminated in Britain and abroad to promote both the production and the actress. In 1887 the *Washington Post* claimed that Ellen Terry 'has been photographed in more than 350 different poses', a tally that would increase significantly as her career continued.[59] In England she sat for famed photographic studios Elliott and Fry, Herbert Rose Barraud and Alexander Bassano. Each of these companies was distinguished in their own way. In 1882 the *London Standard* announced 'The Queen has honoured Mr. Alexander Bassano with sittings for photographs of her Majesty', whilst Elliott and Fry, founded in 1863 on Baker Street, became one of the most successful nineteenth-century photography studios thanks to a new law which gave copyright protection to photographs for the first time. Essentially this meant that if a photographic studio invited a celebrity to sit for a portrait at no fee, then the studio owned the copyright to the images which could then be sold on to the public for a profit. Once again this was a mutually beneficial relationship, with the sitter gaining publicity whilst the photographic firm could add the name of the distinguished celebrity to their clientele and gained income from the sale of prints. These types of celebrity portraits would be kept on file for many years, often being reissued and republished in publications and the press. They could also take on new forms, evolving from cabinet cards to boudoir prints or, from the late 1890s, picture postcards.

When Terry travelled to New York during her American tours, she would visit Napoleon Sarony and Benjamin Falk, two of Manhattan's leading

Opposite: (Figure 42) Unknown photographer, *Ladies of the London Stage*, 1875. Woodburytype. National Portrait Gallery

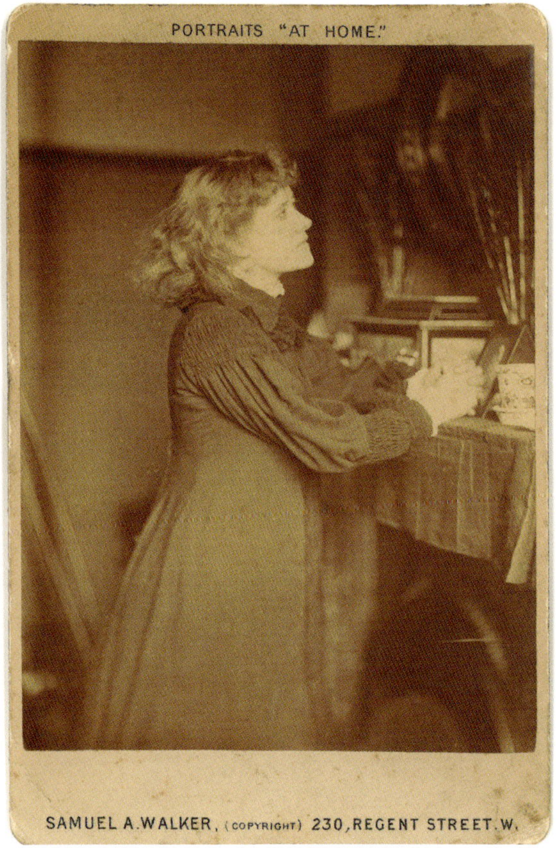

theatrical portrait photographers. Sarony in particular is feted for his cabinet cards of stage personalities. He often courted famous actors and actresses, such as Sarah Bernhardt to whom he offered $1,500 'if the talented actress will permit him the sole right of taking portraits during her brief stay' in New York.[60] Sarony also created numerous enduring images of Ellen Terry in both on- and off-stage clothing (Figure 41), and recalled her as one of his favourite sitters in an interview with the *Los Angeles Times* in 1893. Like so many others, he too, despite being exposed to so many celebrities, had been 'charmed with her'.[61] Sarony's studio, which was established in 1866, produced tens of thousands of cabinet-sized portraits of celebrities which were carefully mounted on gilt-edged card and conspicuously signed by the photographer in the lower left-hand corner. They became highly sought after consumer products that could be bought at Sarony's Union Square studio, or were sold by salesmen in theatres, hotels and through mail-order.[62] In addition, the photographs taken by English studios were exported to dealers in foreign cities. David Mayer has noted how Herbert Rose Barraud exported pictures of his sitters to the New York dealer Dr. Joshua Roth at 5 Union Square, meaning that often 'foreign actresses arriving in New York might expect their photographs to be already in circulation.'[63] This is certainly the case with Ellen Terry. In 1881, two years before Terry was to undertake her first American tour with Irving, the *New York Tribune* reported on the presence of her image in a photographic store on Broadway.[64] Thus the photograph could be viewed and appreciated by people who had never yet had the opportunity to see the actress perform on stage.

That the photographic portrait occupied a prominent place in Victorian society is substantiated by the many references to photographs which appear in contemporary literature and the press. Ellen Terry herself recognised the value and currency of the photograph. An exchange with fellow actress Mary Anderson, which is recorded in Terry's memoirs, recounts how the two women would send each other their most recent photographic portraits. Mary writes to Ellen: 'The last time we met I promised you a photo – here it is! One of my latest! And won't you send me one of yours in private dress? DO!'[65] Ellen would indeed frequently send her latest photographic portrait to friends, such as the American Mrs. Henry W. Beecher, to whom she mailed her picture in 1889, as well as signing photographs for fans after performances. Ellen's requests for photographs of her friends evidences Shearer West's claim that 'Terry examined photographs most carefully and ... engaged with them in a highly personal way.'[66] In 1895, Washington-based newspaper the *Morning Times* relayed to readers Terry's fondness for photographs, documenting how she took a leather case of family photographs with her wherever she travelled.[67] These personal exchanges were just one small part of the great circulation of photographs of Ellen during the latter half of the nineteenth century. A nice example of this is the Sarony portrait, originally taken in Union Square in Manhattan, that found its way to Smallhythe Place, Ellen's home in Kent (Figure 41).

Not only did photography enhance celebrity, it also 'enabled fashion to travel further and faster.'[68] Before the advent of newspaper photography, commercially produced *cartes de visite* and the later cabinet card enabled people to recognise current celebrities and to copy their clothes or manner of wearing them. Through photographic portraits Ellen Terry's particular style of Aesthetic clothing – whether stage costumes or her own personal garments – was projected to an ever-widening audience. Photographs of the actress were not only collected by adoring fans, but from the 1880s were reproduced with increasing frequency in the press.

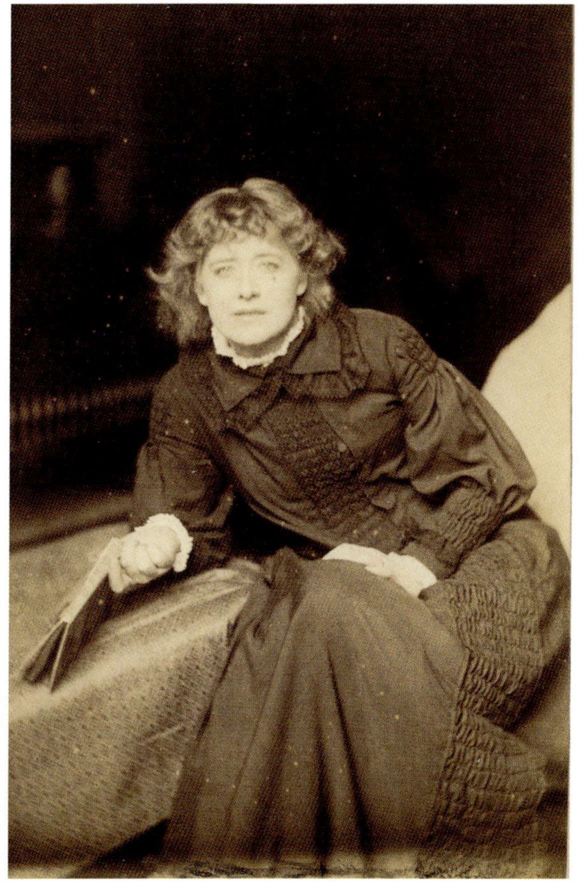

Opposite: (Figure 43) Samuel Alexander Walker, *Ellen Terry at Home*, c.1873. Cabinet card. Smallhythe Place, National Trust

Above: (Figure 44) Samuel Alexander Walker, *Ellen Terry at Home,* c.1873. Cabinet card. Smallhythe Place, National Trust

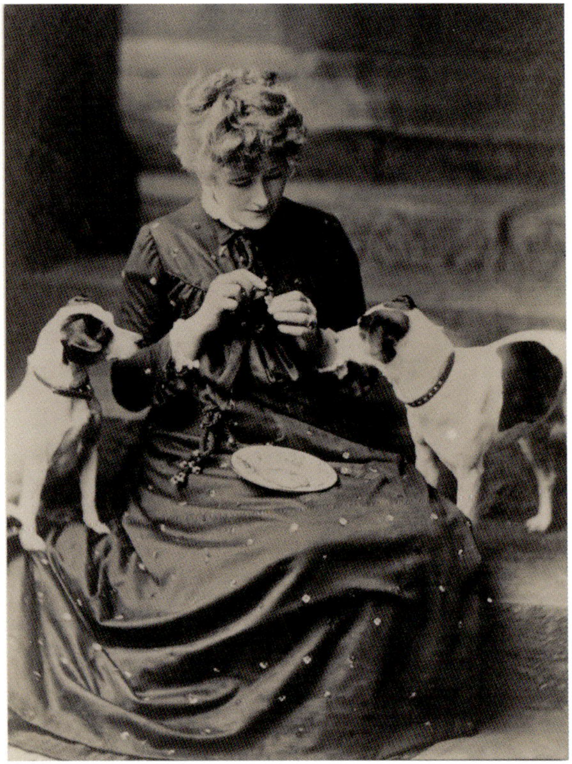

Above: (Figure 45) William Henry Grove, *Ellen Terry*, 1889. Vintage bromide postcard print. National Portrait Gallery

Opposite: (Figure 46) Window & Grove, *Ellen Terry as Camma in 'The Cup'*, 1881. Photograph. Smallhythe Place, National Trust

The ability of the cabinet card to communicate information on Aesthetic dress styles worn by Terry rendered it similar to the fashion plate. A group of portraits of the actress taken by the photographer Samuel Alexander Walker depict her in personal clothing (Figure 43 & 44). Although all the images are undated, it is likely that they were taken in the 1870s when Ellen was living with E. W. Godwin. By this date Godwin had exerted a profound influence on Ellen's tastes in art and decoration, and had taught her the modes of an Aesthetic lifestyle. Ellen herself recalls how during this period her style had not a trace of the fashion of the time and that her appearance could elicit surprise from visitors.[69] The photographs form part of Walker's *Portraits at Home* series, in which sitters were photographed in domestic settings. These prints were popular with the public and publicised by *The Era* in July 1880, which reported: 'Mr S. A. Walker has most attractively ministered to the popular taste in his beautiful series of portraits at home.' The article praises the photographs of Miss Terry, which have been arranged in a most 'artistic and graceful manner', where 'the lady looks her very best.'[70] Such intimate portraits served to bring Terry closer to the public, and in particular to female fans who could carefully study details of her garments. The three cabinet cards portray Terry in various manifestations of Aesthetic dress. One depicts her wearing a Japanese kimono, with a wide obi-style sash tied around the waist and with hanging sleeves (Figure 48). In her right hand Terry holds the quintessential Aesthetic accessory, an Oriental fan. The cabinet card is evidence of Terry's experimentation with clothing off stage, her dedication to wearing unconventional styles of dress and her alignment with the Aesthetic Movement, which upheld Japanese design for its beautiful simplicity. The other two cabinet cards show her wearing an Aesthetic smocked garment, in this instance a Mother Hubbard gown (Figures 43 & 44). This was another form of loose-fitting and

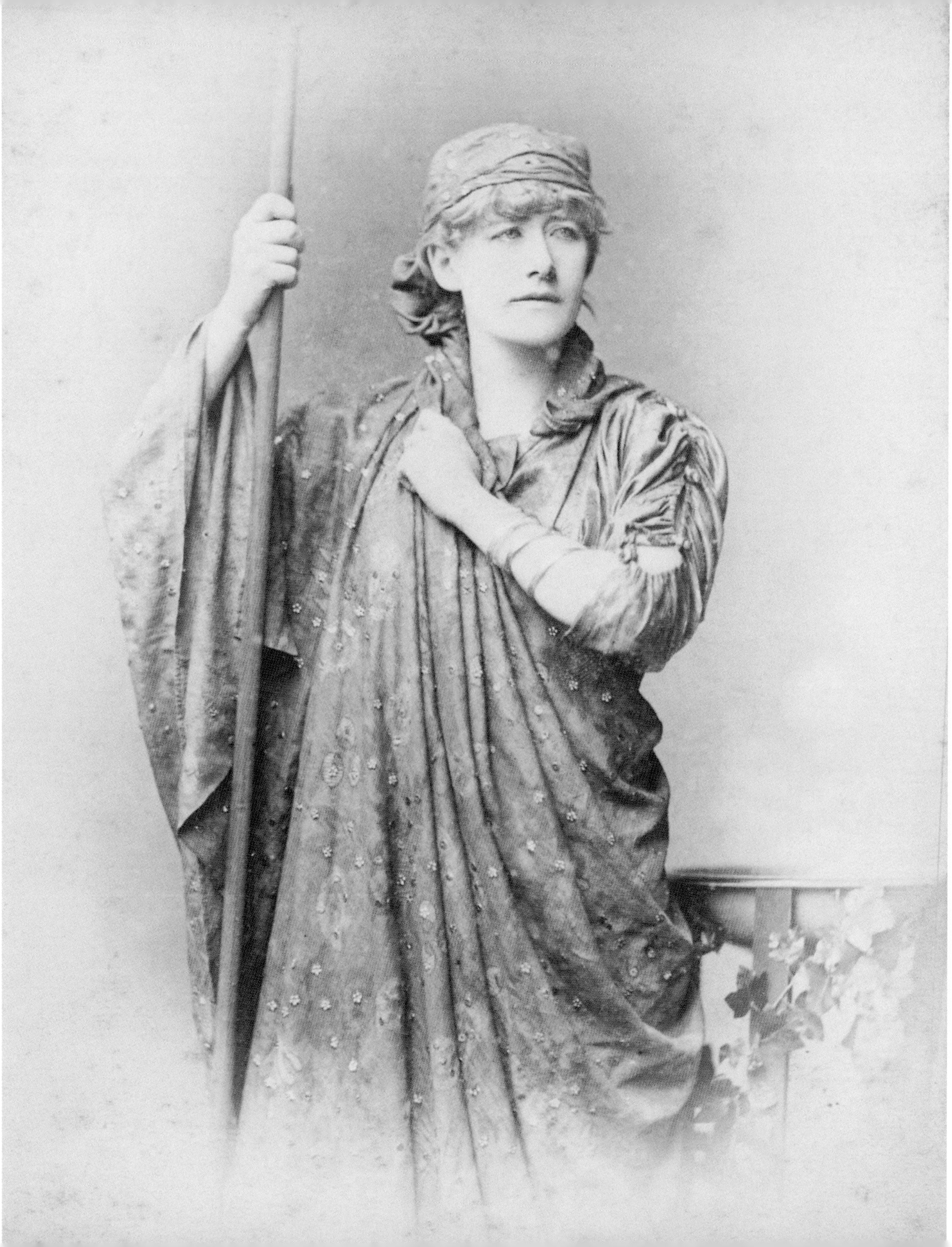

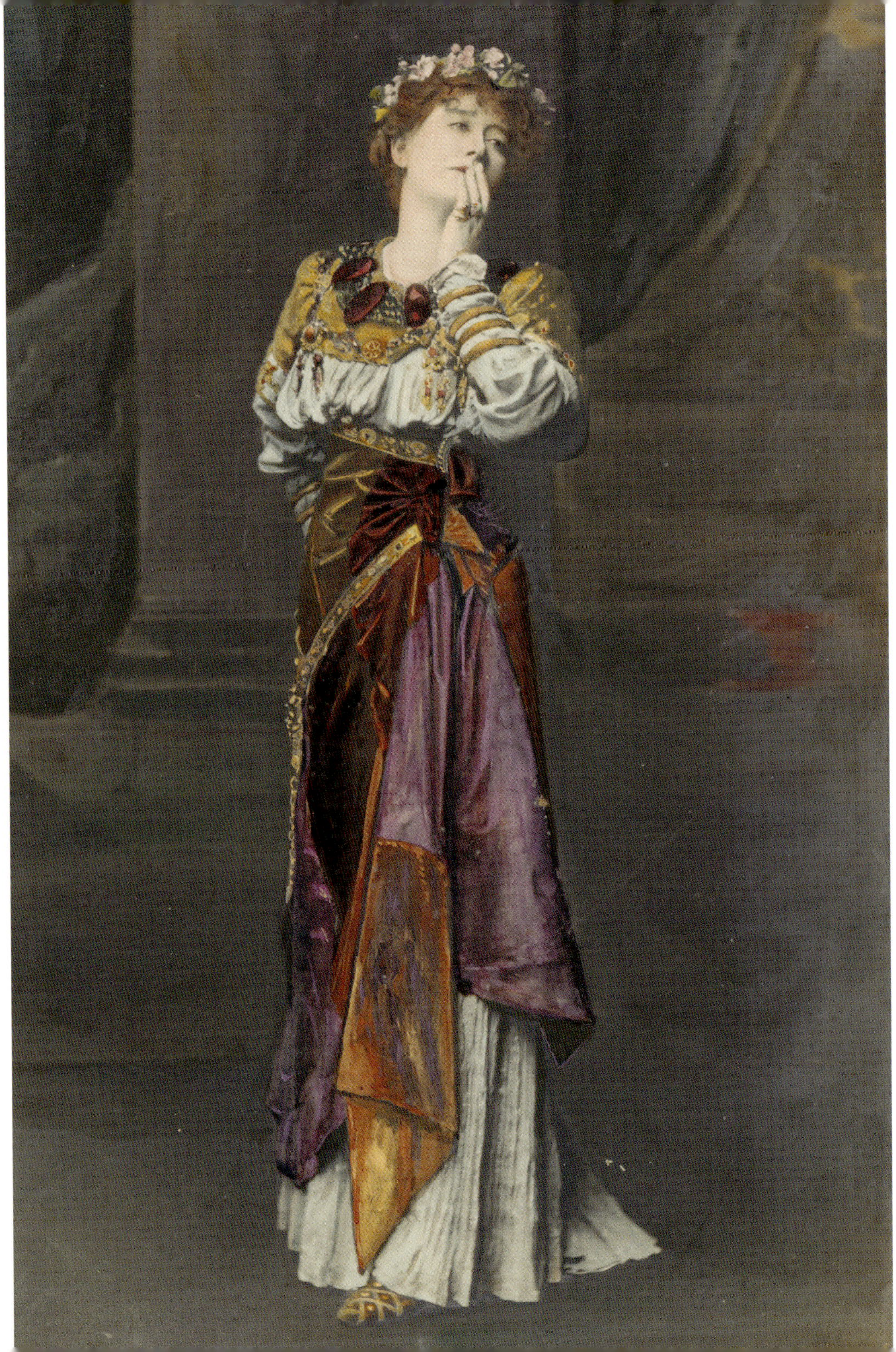

uncorseted dress that was essentially a round-yoke wrapper which could be worn belted or left loose. The dress is clearly worn without a corset and is made from a plain, probably cotton fabric. Understated small white frills adorn the neckline and cuffs. This dress also features shirring at the yoke and wrist, and its fuller, slightly puffed sleeves and the high-standing ruffled collar of her smock underneath add a historicising element. Smocking and shirring were distinctive features of Aesthetic dress and were prominent characteristics of many of Terry's personal garments. As Patricia Cunningham has observed, 'a loose garment smocked at the neck, wrist, and waist offered considerably more ease and flexibility than the fashionable stiff, heavily boned dresses, which also required a stiffened corset.'[71] Terry chose to wear this type of Aesthetic dress frequently in her photographic portraits (Figure 45). In keeping with *Harper's Bazaar's* definition of Aesthetic dress, the garments in all these photographs are 'above all things, flowing, unrestrained' and 'free from the tyranny of the present burden of kilted flounces, fixed draperies, and tie back skirts.'[72] Furthermore, and perhaps most importantly, they promoted the individual taste of the wearer and demonstrated Terry's disregard for conventional fashion, which favoured far more complicated toilettes. A comparison with cabinet cards depicting fashions worn by two of her female contemporaries, French actress Jane Hading and professional beauty/actress Lillie Langtry, reveals the subversive nature of Terry's personal style, which differed in both shape and form, as well as material. Whilst Hading and Langtry are tightly encased and wearing bustles, Terry favoured soft lines in her dresses and gave preference to light fabrics such as poplin, wool and cashmere as opposed to the heavy and highly trimmed fabrics that were popular during the 1880s.

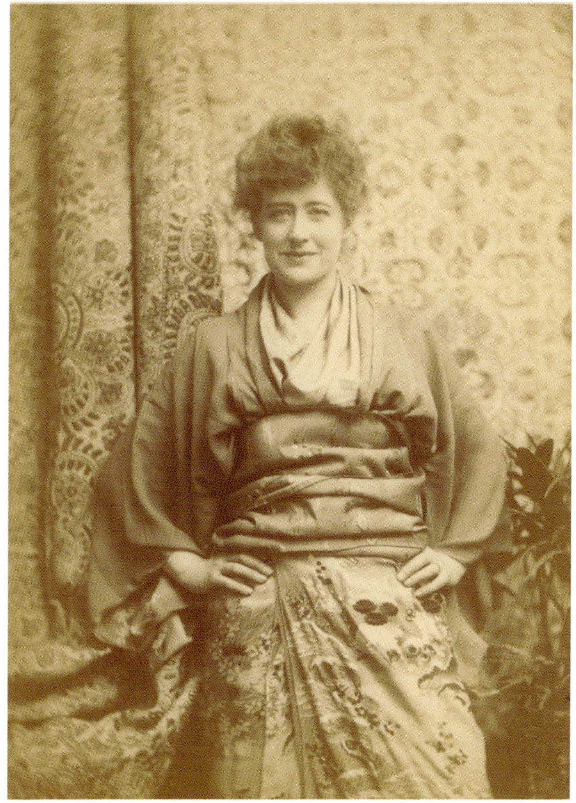

Opposite: (Figure (47) Window & Grove, *Miss Ellen Terry as Imogen in 'Cymbeline'*, c. 1896. Hand coloured photograph. Smallhythe Place, National Trust

Above: (Figure 48) Samuel Alexander Walker, *Ellen Terry as a Japanese Lady*, 1875. Photograph/cabinet card. Smallhythe Place, National Trust

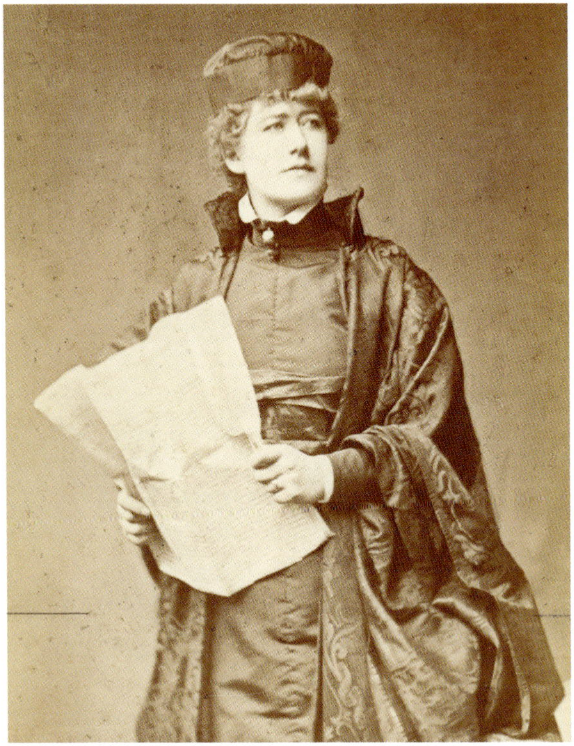

Above: (Figure 49) Window & Grove, *Ellen Terry as Portia in 'The Merchant of Venice'*, 1879. Photograph. Smallhythe Place, National Trust

Opposite: (Figure 50) Window & Grove, *Ellen Terry as Guinevere in 'King Arthur'*, 1895. Albumen cabinet card. National Portrait Gallery

Many of Terry's theatrical costumes were a natural extension of the actress's own artistic and aesthetic tastes.[73] Indeed her on- and off-stage clothed appearance was often interchangeable, and many of the gowns Terry wore in Lyceum productions related to her personal clothing. Costume was of course integral to Terry's theatrical performances and enabled her to create a beautiful pictorial effect on the stage. She exerted considerable control over her stage wardrobe and used costumes to complement her natural acting style, preferring light and unrestrictive garments that allowed her to move freely about the stage. In her memoirs she discusses her careful consideration of stage costume in relation to the overall production, stating: 'I have always been friendly with the scene-painters, perhaps because I have always taken pains about my dresses, and consulted them beforehand about the colour, so that I should not look wrong in their scenes, nor their scenes wrong with my dresses.'[74] In 1894 *McClure's Magazine* noted the importance of costuming to the actress:

> No detail in the accessories of the part she creates escapes her interest, and she has strong theories on the subject of wherewithal she shall be clothed. The character should find expression in the costume, according to Miss Terry, and she bestows endless thought upon the introduction of apparent trifles, notes in harmony with the individuality of the woman she portrays.[75]

As Valerie Cumming has noted, 'Ellen Terry was a beautiful woman, a fine actress and a shrewd professional assessor of what dresses, in performance and in private, would captivate and delight her public.'[76] This meant an astute appreciation and realisation of picturesque Aesthetic dress that Terry promoted both on stage and in her photographic portraits, an emphasis perhaps best summed up by an article in the *New York Tribune* which profiled the actress's

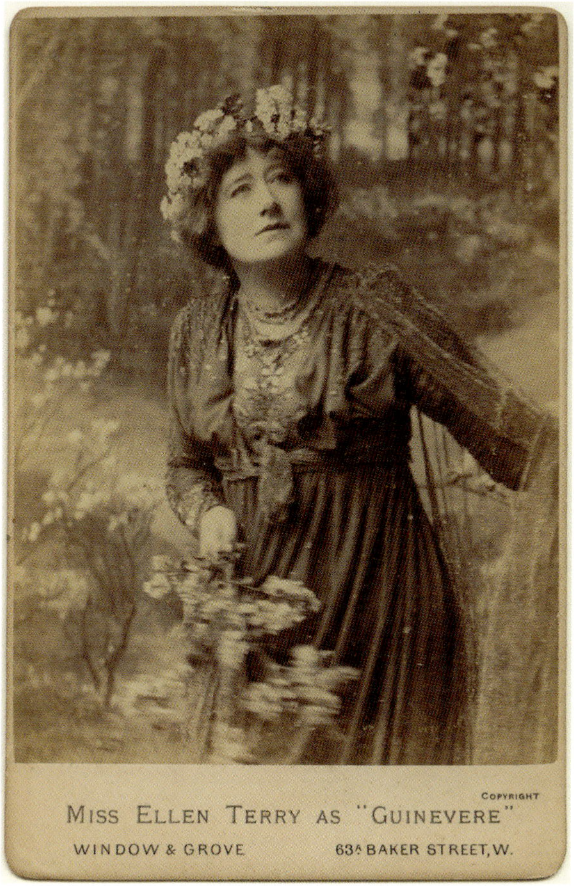

style for its readers: 'She simply wears "aesthetic" garments because the classic folds become her lily-like face and slender figure.'[77]

Classical dress from Antiquity was an important source of inspiration for aesthetes and many of Terry's stage costumes and elements of her private dress feature artistically draped fabric. The appeal of Classical dress lay in its beautiful simplicity, with drapery allowing free and graceful disposition of the limbs. The qualities of this type of dress were evident in Terry's rendition of Camma in the Lyceum's 1881 production of Tennyson's *The Cup*. Full-length and seated portraits of Terry wearing Grecian robes for this role (designed by Godwin) demonstrate her skill at giving life to drapery (Figure 46). The overall effect was highly praised by a reporter from the *Hampshire Advertiser*: 'There is certainly no actress, even in this age of excessive stage dressiness, who appears in finer or more costly costumes, or who wears these costumes with better grace than Miss Ellen Terry. Her Iolanthe and her Portia were both remarkable in this respect. In The Cup she surpasses herself.'[78] Artful use of drapery was again emphasised in the gowns Ellen wore for the role of Imogen in the 1896 production of *Cymbeline*. The artist Lawrence Alma-Tadema, known for his Classically-inspired paintings, designed both the scenery and costumes for this production. The dress executed by Mrs Nettleship (Figure 47) is described in Ellen's memoirs as one of the loveliest she ever wore.[79] *Harper's Bazaar* described this garment in great detail, praising its beautifully draped construction:

> It is arranged in the tiniest pleats from throat to hem, and would apparently hang loosely from the neck, only that a sort of over-skirt drapery confines the waist, and the pleated blue silk hangs a little over this over-skirt in a loose blouse effect ... it gradually dawns upon you that the drapery is like an octave on the piano – the tone scarcely different from one to another note, and yet in a moment you have the vast difference of an octave.[80]

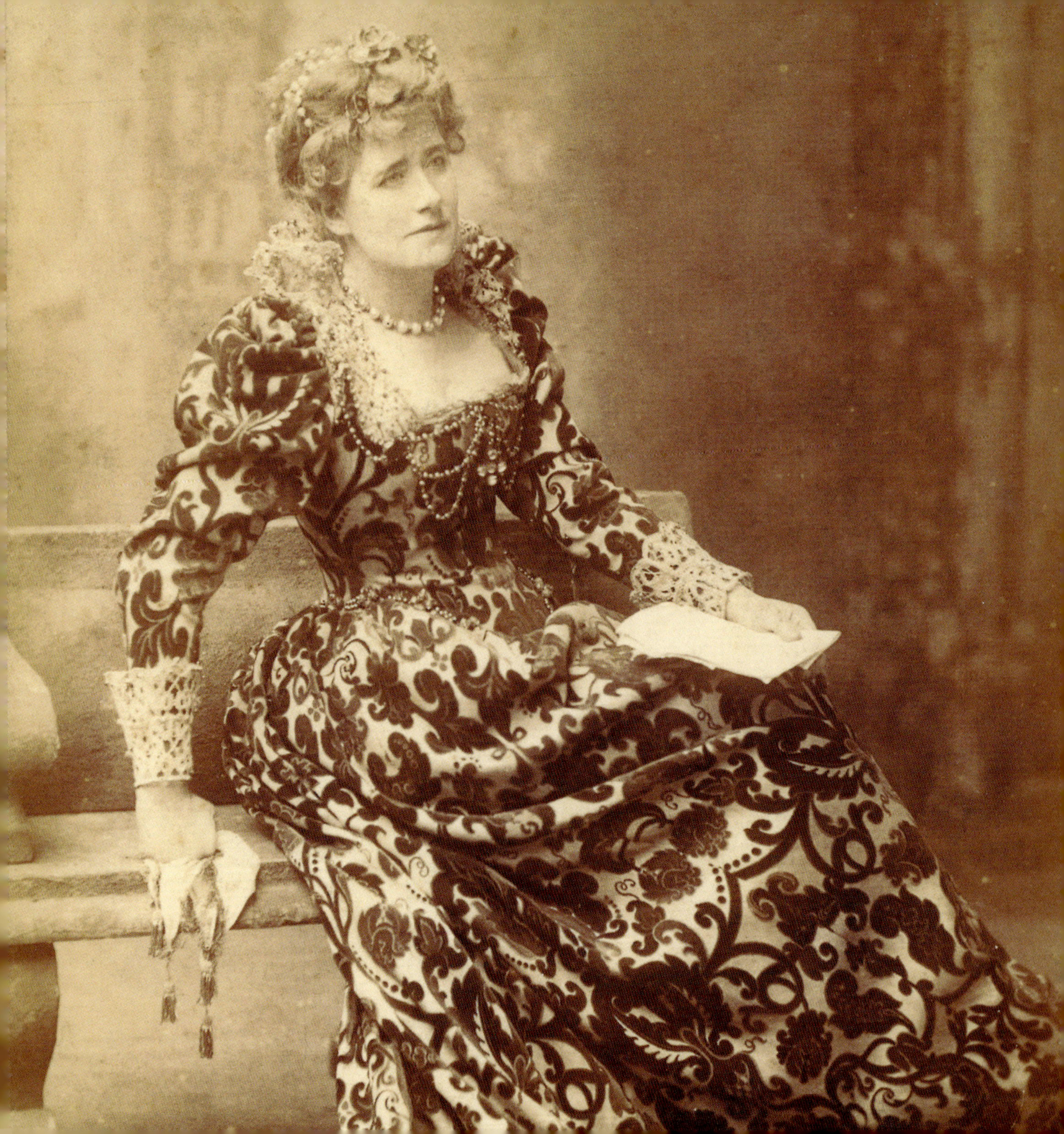

It was also a costume that diverged radically from conventional fashion, which at this date celebrated an hourglass silhouette with wide skirt and exaggerated ballooning sleeves.

In their quest for achieving beauty in dress, aesthetes often looked to the past for inspiration, allying their style with historicism.[81] In the process, they rejected many elements of mainstream fashion, and instead promoted earlier styles of dress that were felt to better reveal the natural beauty of the human form and which allowed the wearer to apply the principles of art to dress. Through her stage costumes and by extension her photographic portraits, Terry was an important figure in popularising historical modes of dress. Dress historian Aileen Ribeiro notes how 'lavish theatrical productions such as those by Henry Irving and the Lyceum also served to fuel an interest in the "glamour" of the historical past.'[82] For those who could not attend these productions, Terry's photographic portraits served to reproduce her inimitable stage costumes and offered a means for women to study the historical and artistic elements of her garments. Examining cabinet cards of the actress, we can observe that Medieval and Renaissance details featured prominently in several of her stage dresses. Among those that were in keeping with *Harper's Bazaar's* dictum that anything decidedly 'old-fashioned' was artistic, were the quasi-Renaissance dresses she wore for the role of Portia in the Lyceum's 1879 sell-out production of *The Merchant of Venice* and for Beatrice in *Much Ado About Nothing* a few years later (Figure 49 & 51). For both roles she wore similar dresses of rich brocade, featuring a square neckline, voluminous sleeves and Medici collar, allowing her to create a picturesque appearance that could be said to chime with the Aesthetic Movement's notion of using dress to please the eye and to create a beauty that mesmerised and enchanted the beholder. That these stage dresses captivated the public is affirmed by the many complimentary press reviews. *The Aberdeen Journal* quoted an article from the American *Ladies' Gazette of Fashion* in which a journalist wrote that 'Miss Ellen Terry's dresses are remarkable for their beauty of material and their good taste in her representation of Portia at the Lyceum.' Long descriptions of the gowns follow and the article ends with the journalist declaring that 'the effect of both these dresses is so good that I feel sure we shall see them copied for evening costumes during the coming season, taste for historical costumes being as pronounced as ever.'[83]

Opposite: (Figure 51) Window & Grove, *Miss Ellen Terry as Beatrice*, 1882. Photograph. Smallhythe Place, National Trust

Medieval influence is especially evident in gowns that were designed for Terry by Alice Comyns Carr from the mid-1880s. Alice was the wife of Joseph Comyns Carr, the director of the Grosvenor Gallery. She was a prominent figure in the Aesthetic Movement and it has been suggested that she was the model for George Du Maurier's character Mrs Cimabue Brown, the aesthete disciple who appears in his *Punch* cartoons. Carr became a close friend of Terry's and was responsible for some of her most successful stage costumes, including the famous and highly publicised beetle-wing dress worn for the role of Lady Macbeth. Although Terry's novel interpretation of Lady Macbeth in 1888 may have divided critics in Britain and America, all were unanimous in their

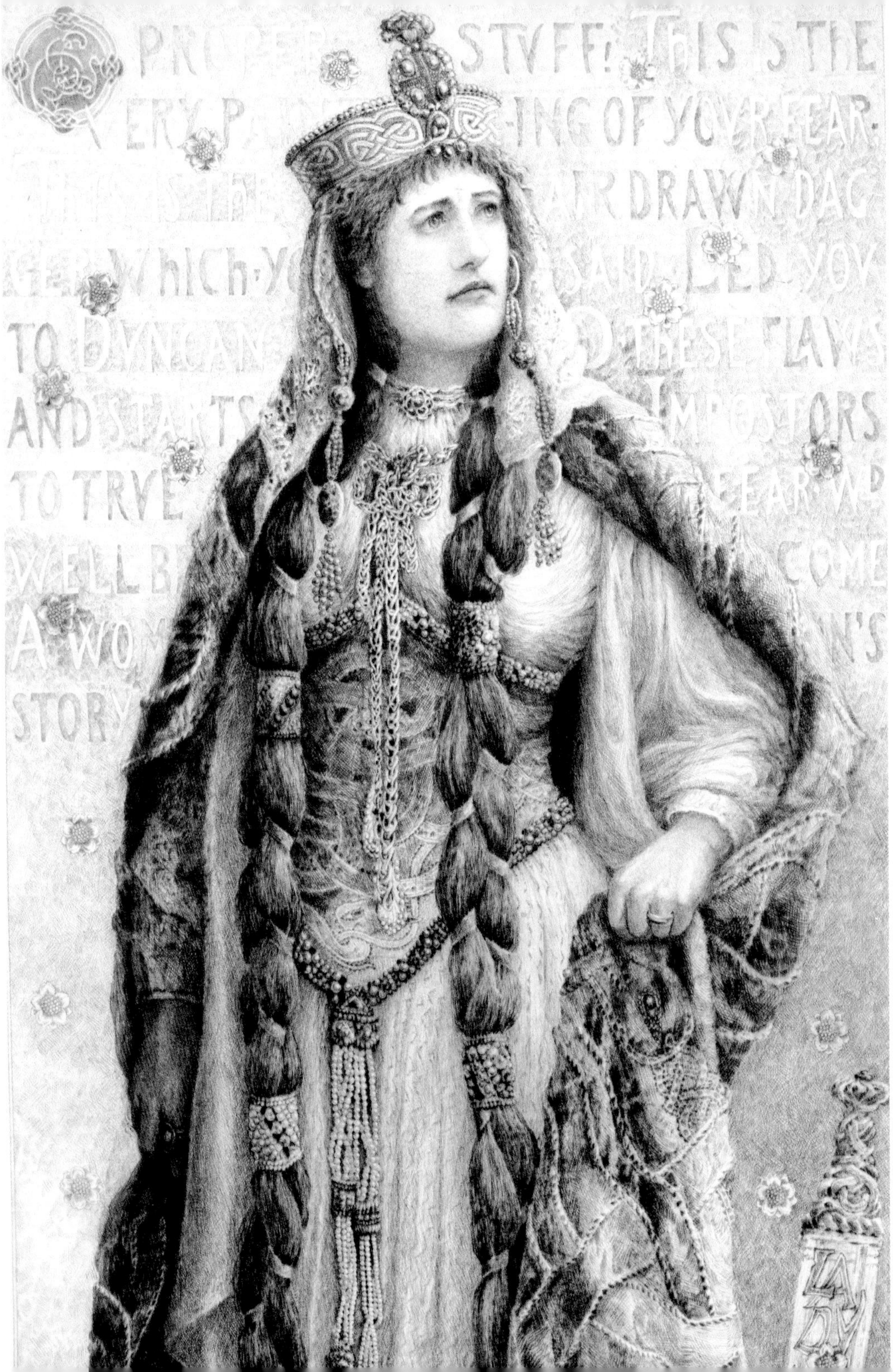
STVFF! THIS IS THE
ING OF YOVR FEAR
DRAWN DAG
SAID LED YOV
TO DVNCAN
THESE FLAWS
AND STARTS
IMPOSTORS
TO TRVE
COME
STORY

praise for her stunning costumed appearance (Figure 53). *The New York Times* noted that 'her dressing of the part is extremely attractive, in quaintly, archaic, flowing variations of Saxon costume.'[84] Meanwhile, the *Manchester Weekly Times* went so far as to suggest that 'Ellen Terry's costumes constitute the central point of interest in the play' and that 'not only are her dresses exquisite, but the other performers "play up" well to the leading actress in this respect, and the combination of colours is often very beautiful.'[85] Other costumes designed by Carr for Terry that are in keeping with the Pre-Raphaelite and later Aesthetic creed that found beauty in the purer lines and colours of early medieval art are those she created for Terry's role as Guinevere in the 1895 production of *King Arthur* (Figure 50), described by *The Era* as being beautiful and 'joys forever in form and colour.'[86]

By examining Ellen Terry's cabinet cards one can see that the actress consistently championed Aesthetic styles of dress on stage and in private. She preferred the unembellished, artistic clothing created by her dressmaker, Mrs Nettleship, to the lavish and extravagantly decorated garments of couturiers such as Charles Frederick Worth. Her stage gowns were equally escapist and rejected many aspects of conventional fashion, adopting the principle that anything old was bound to be better. Alongside laudatory descriptions in newsprint, Terry's attractive appearance in Aesthetic garments in photographic portraits heightened the charm of such clothing to the female public. In 1889 the *Manchester Weekly Times* commented: 'the stage has always had some influence upon the costumes of the moment, but

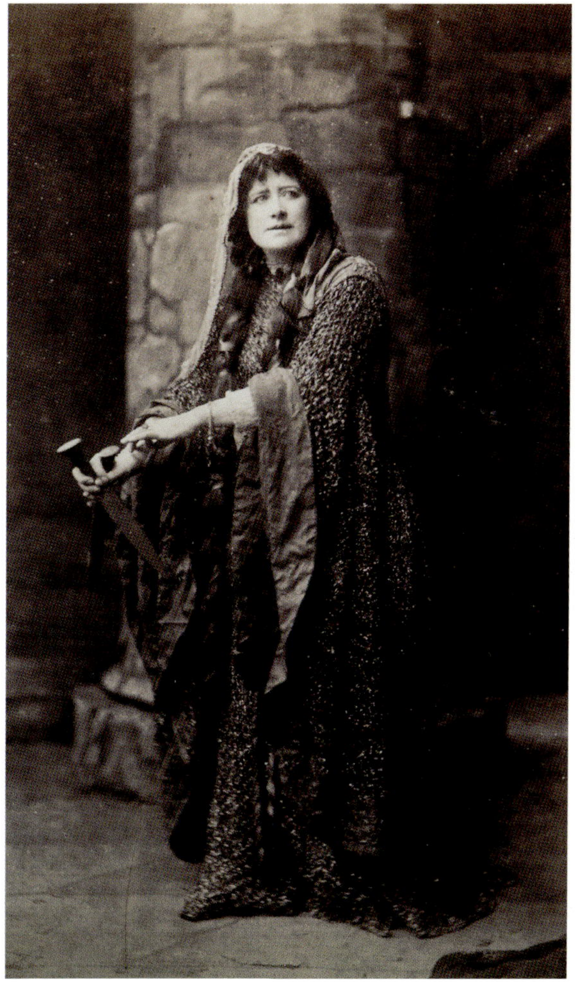

Opposite: (Figure 53) Henry Batley, *Ellen Terry as Lady Macbeth*, 1889. Etching. Watts Gallery

Above: (Figure 52) Window & Grove, *Ellen Terry as Lady Macbeth*, c.1888. Photograph. Smallhythe Place, National Trust

now it is taking a new form, that of encouraging individuality in dress.'[87] Through sartorial choices documented in her portrait photographs, Ellen offered women the possibility of experimenting with clothing as a means of self-expression. By recognising the sense of potential and liberation that the photographs of Ellen were thereby able to communicate, we are able to understand the huge charisma that these mass-produced images projected. Reporting in the 'Ladies' Column' of the *Leicester Chronicle*, a female journalist extolled the appeal of Terry's photographs:

> How lovely all female beauty or even female plainness looks when perpetuated by Window and Grove, or Elliott and Fry ... The photographs just produced of Ellen Terry as Portia, with a tapestry background, are extremely beautiful. Her pictures have been particularly successful and charming as Ophelia also, and those who admire her cannot do better than secure some of them from Window and Grove, which are, I think, quite the best.[88]

In 1885 the *Belfast Newsletter*, reporting on the craze for celebrity portraiture, declared:

> There are, it would seem, certain personages of whose pictorial representations the world cannot have enough. It will have the same individuals in all sorts of attitudes and dresses. It will have them in the form of photographs, or prints, or pictures in the illustrated papers.[89]

Ellen Terry was one of the first superstars of the mass-produced photographic portrait. She was photographed throughout her life by commercial studios, leaving us with an extensive record of her achievements on stage, as well as by artistic photographers, such as Julia Margaret Cameron and Frederick Hollyer, whose photographs offer a more personal and intimate insight into the legendary actress. A sketch by the artist and illustrator Pamela Coleman Smith depicts the pioneer female press photographer Kate Pragnell in her studio standing at her camera with three photographs of Ellen Terry in the background (Figure 54). The sketch encapsulates the popularity and currency of Ellen's image. Pragnell had opened a studio in London in the 1890s where many society ladies would come to have their portraits taken for the publication *Hearth and Home*. The display of Terry's photographic portrait in the studio would have served as a reminder of the great actress's many poses and famous photographic portraits. For her part, Pamela Coleman Smith – a member of Ellen's own intimate circle – points up the strangeness that a 'celebrity portrait' must have for one who knows the sitter well as a real person. Photographic images of Ellen Terry were to be found throughout the visual culture of the late nineteenth century. They represented a meeting place of theatre, fashion and art; they were a point of contact between a cultural élite and the innumerable women who studied Ellen's portraits as windows to a more beautiful, more liberated world; and they were, finally, enigmatic clues to the complex personality of one of the great Victorian performers.

Opposite: (Figure 54) Pamela Colman Smith, *Kate Pragnell*, 1900. Watercolour with ink and graphite underdrawing. Smallhythe Place, National Trust

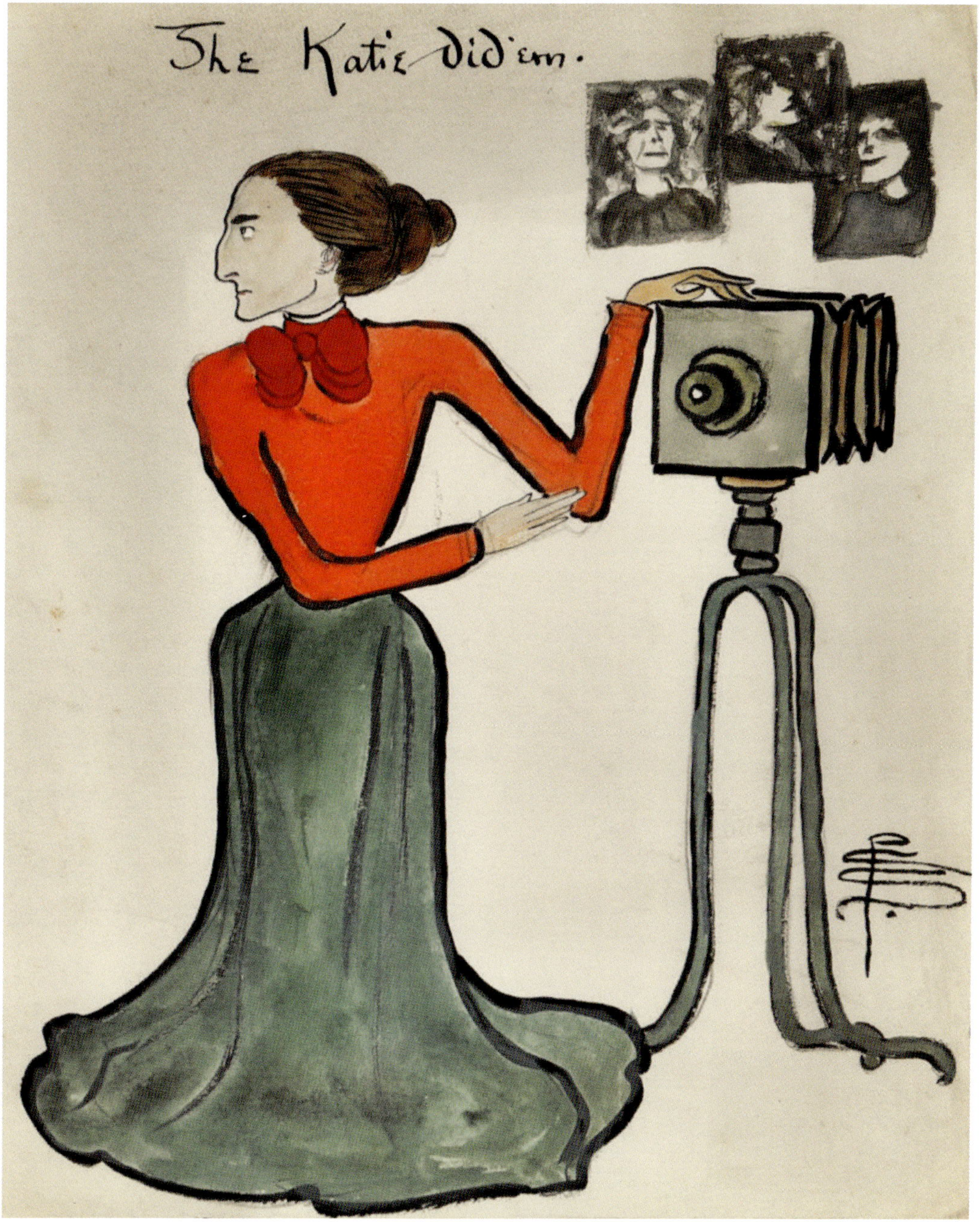

The Katie did'em.

References

Adam, Eve, ed., *Mrs J. Comyns Carr's Reminiscences* (London: Hutchinson, 1926)

Auerbach, Nina, *Ellen Terry: Player in Her Time* (London: Dent, 1987)

Barrington, Emilie, *G.F. Watts. Reminiscences* (London: George Allen, 1905)

Bassham, Ben L., *The Theatrical Photographs of Napoleon Sarony* (Kent OH: Kent State University Press, 1978)

Bryant, Barbara, *G. F. Watts Portraits: Fame and Beauty in Victorian Society* (London: National Portrait Gallery, 2004)

Calloway, Stephen and Lynn Federle Orr, eds, *The Cult of Beauty: The Aesthetic Movement 1860-1900* (London: V&A Publishing, 2011)

Cockin, Katharine, ed., *The Collected Letters of Ellen Terry*, 4 vols (London: Pickering & Chatto, 2010)

Cox, Julian and Colin Ford, *Julia Margaret Cameron: The Complete Photographs* (London: Thames & Hudson, 2003)

Craig, Edith and Christopher St John, eds, *Ellen Terry's Memoirs* (London: Gollancz, 1933)

Craig, Edward Gordon, *Ellen Terry and her Secret Self* (London: Sampson, Low, Marston, 1931)

Craig, Edward Gordon, Gordon *Craig: The Story of his Life* (London: Gollancz, 1968)

Cumming, Valerie, 'Ellen Terry: An Aesthetic Actress and her Costumes', *Costume,* 21: 1 (1987): 67-74

Cunningham, Patricia A., *Reforming Women's Fashion, 1850-1920: Politics, Health and Art* (Kent OH: Kent State University Press, 2003)

Franklin Gould, Veronica, *G. F. Watts, The Last Great Victorian* (New Haven and London: Yale University Press, 2004)

Franklin Gould, Veronica, *The Vision of G. F. Watts* (Compton: Watts Gallery, 2004)

Franklin Gould, Veronica, *Tennyson at Farringford* (Freshwater: Farringford House Press, 2009)

Franklin Gould, Veronica, 'Ellen Terry and G. F. Watts: "Blasted with Ecstasy"', in Katharine Cochin, ed., *Ellen Terry: Spheres of Influence* (London: Pickering & Chatto, 2011)

Gernsheim, Helmut, *Julia Margaret Cameron: Her Life and Photographic Work* (London: Gordon Fraser, 1975)

Green, Roger Lancelyn, ed., *The Diaries of Lewis Carroll,* 2 vols (London: Cassell, 1953-54)

Hamilton, Peter and Roger Hargreaves, *The Beautiful and the Damned: The Creation of Identity in Nineteenth-Century Photography* (Aldershot: Lund Humphries, 2001)

Hannavy, John, ed., *Encyclopedia of Nineteenth-Century Photography* (London: Routledge, 2008)

Harbron, Dudley, *The Conscious Stone: The Life of Edward William Godwin* (London: Latimer House, 1949)

Haweis, Mary Eliza, *The Art of Beauty* (London: Chatto & Windus, 1878)

Hiatt, Charles, *Ellen Terry and Her Impersonations: An Appreciation* (London: George Bell, 1898)

Holroyd, Michael, *A Strange Eventful History. The Dramatic Lives of Ellen Terry, Henry Irving and their Remarkable Families* (London: Vintage, 2009)

Jopling, Louise, *Twenty Years of My Life, 1867 to 1887* (London: John Lane, 1925)

Levitt, Sarah, *Fashion in Photographs*, 1880-1900 (London: Batsford, 1991)

Loshak, David, 'G. F. Watts and Ellen Terry', *Burlington Magazine*, 105: 728 (November 1963): 476-87

Manvell, Roger, *Ellen Terry: A Biography* (London: Heinemann, 1968)

Mayer, David, 'The Actress as Photographic Icon: from Early Photography to Early Film,' in

Maggie B. Gale & John Stokes, eds, *The Cambridge Companion to the Actress* (Cambridge: Cambridge University Press, 2007)

Melville, Joy, *Ellen Terry* (London: Haus, 2006)

Merritt, Anna Lea, *Love Locked Out: The Memoirs of Anna Lea Merritt*, ed. Galina Gorokhoff (Boston MA: Museum of Fine Arts, 1982)

Ormond, Richard and Elaine Kilmurray, *John Singer Sargent: The Early Portraits* (New Haven and London: Yale University Press, 1998)

Ribeiro, Aileen, 'Fashion and Whistler', in *Whistler, Women and Fashion,* eds Margaret F. Macdonald, Susan Grace Galassi and Aileen Ribeiro with Patricia de Montfort (New Haven and London: Yale University Press, 2003)

Robertson, W. Graham, *Time Was* [1931] (London: Quartet, 1981)

St John, Christopher, ed., *Shaw–Terry: A Correspondence* (London: Constable, 1931)

Squire, Geoffrey, *Simply Stunning: The Pre-Raphaelite Art of Dressing* (Cheltenham: Art Gallery and Museums, 1996)

Steen, Marguerite, *A Pride of Terrys. Family Saga* (London: Longmans, 1962)

Stoker, Bram, *Personal Reminiscences of Henry Irving*, 2 vols (London: Heinemann, 1906)

Stokes, John, Michael R. Booth and Susan Bassnett, eds, *Bernhardt, Terry, Duse: The Actress in her Time* (Cambridge: Cambridge University Press, 1988)

Terry, Ellen, *The Story of My Life* [1908] (New York: Schocken Books, 1982)

Terry, Ellen, *Four Lectures on Shakespeare* (London: Hopkinson, 1932)

Vicinus, Martha, ed., *A Widening Sphere: Changing Roles of Victorian Women* (Bloomington IN: Indiana University Press, 1977)

Watts, Mary Seton, *George Frederic Watts: The Annals of an Artist's Life*, 3 vols (London: Macmillan, 1912).

West, Shearer, 'The Photographic Portraiture of Henry Irving and Ellen Terry', in Anselm Heinrich, Kate Newey and Jeffrey Richards, eds, *Ruskin, the Theatre and Victorian Visual Culture* (Basingstoke: Palgrave Macmillan, 2009)

Wilde, Oscar, *Works* (Ware: Wordsworth, 1994)

Endnotes

1 Charles Dickens to William Macready, 19 February 1863 (Kate Terry album, V&A, f.5).
2 *Times*, 1 May 1856, 9; Green, I, 88; Craig and St John, 16.
3 Craig and St John, 34.
4 *Ibid,* 38.
5 *Times*, 22 June 1863.
6 Barrington, 100-1.
7 *Isaiah* XXI: 11-12.
8 Barrington, 35.
9 *Hamlet*, I, iii.
10 G. F. Watts to Constance Leslie, 1864 (Leslie Papers, Castle Leslie, K/6/1); to J. P Martineau, 13 December 1876 (Watts Gallery archive); St John, xv; Craig and St John, 40.
11 Craig 1931, 22; Craig and St John, 43 and 51.
12 Franklin Gould 2009, 55-56.
13 Gernsheim, 84.
14 Quoted in Gernsheim, 79.
15 Barrington, 35.
16 St John, xi.
17 Craig and St John, 42.
18 *Hamlet*, I, iii.
19 *Times*, 30 April 1864, 14.
20 National Archives, COPY 1/6/941 30 June 1864; Cox and Ford, 267-69.
21 Craig and St. John, 41 and 44-45.
22 Barrington, 36.
23 Auerbach, 17.
24 Cockin, I, 1.
25 *Athenaeum*, 6 May 1865.
26 Loshak, fig.19.
27 Franklin Gould, *Vision of G. F. Watts,* 22-23 and 73.
28 *Art Journal*, 1868, 110; Franklin Gould, *G. F. Watts*, 90-91 and *Vision of G. F. Watts*, 42-43, 58.
29 Holroyd, 1-2.
30 Terry 1932, 165.
31 Cockin, I, letter 133.
32 Craig and St John, 120-21.
33 Wilde, 840; Craig and St John, 140 and 155.
34 Craig and St John, 162.
35 Stoker, I, 101.

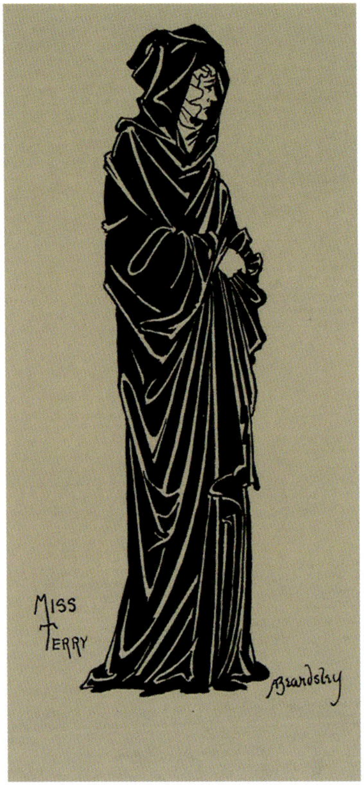

Above: (Figure 55) Aubrey Beardsley, *Ellen Terry as Rosamund de Clifford in Tennyson's 'Becket',* c.1893. Print on paper. Smallhythe Place, National Trust

Opposite (Figure 56) Pamela Colman Smith, *Ellen Terry as Portia hurrying to the Railway Station*, 9 December 1900. Print on paper. Smallhythe Place, National Trust

36 Franklin Gould, *G. F. Watts*, 172-79, *Vision of G. F. Watts*, 65.
37 Stoker, 192-93; Cockin, I, 81; Franklin Gould, *G. F. Watts*,195.
38 Craig and St John, 233-35; Adam, 211-12; Cockin, II, letter 312.
39 *Ibid*, 240; Adam, 205-8 and 254.
40 *Ibid,* 253, 256-57.
41 *Ibid*, 275-76.
42 Robertson, 54.
43 St John, 213.
44 Terry to Lady Constance Leslie (Leslie Papers, Castle Leslie, K/6/1); Cockin, IV, letter 1353; Stoker, 200 and 207.
45 Mayer, 88.
46 'Miss Ellen Terry', *Shields Daily Gazette*, 24 November 1894.
47 Calloway and Orr, 11.
48 Terry 1982, 68.
49 Melville, 27.
50 Hiatt, 254-55.
51 Terry 1982, 96.
52 John Plunkett, 'Celebrity and Royalty' in Hannavy, 277.
53 'Marion's Illustrated Calling Cards', *London Daily News*, 1 September 1858.
54 Christopher Kent, 'Image and Reality: The Actress and Society,' in Vicinus, 99.
55 'The Sale of Photographs', *Observer*, 26 October 1879.
56 Hamilton and Hargreaves, 37.
57 *Ibid.*, 43.
58 'Shop Window Celebrity', *Belfast Newsletter,* 14 December 1885.
59 'Personal Intelligence', *Washington Post*, 19 March 1887.
60 'Expensive Photographs', *Portsmouth Evening News*, 15 November 1880.
61 Napoleon Sarony, 'Women and Cameras', *Los Angeles Times*, 26 November 1893.
62 Bassham, 14.
63 Mayer, 85.
64 'The Sale of Photographs', *New York Tribune*, 30 October 1881.
65 Terry 1982, 190.
66 West, 207.
67 'Famous Women as Housekeepers', *Morning Times*, 17 November 1895.
68 Levitt, 14.
69 Terry 1982, 64.
70 'Samuel A. Walker's Portraits at Home', *Era*, 4 July 1880.
71 Cunningham, 114.
72 *Ibid.*
73 Cumming, 69.
74 Terry 1982, 43.
75 Ethel Mackenzie McKenna, 'Ellen Terry', *McClure's Magazine*, April 1894.
76 Cumming, 73.
77 'Irving and Ellen Terry', *New York Tribune*, 9 July 1882.
78 *Hampshire Advertiser County Newspaper*, 15 January 1881.
79 Terry 1982, 224.
80 Bessie O'Connor, 'Ellen Terry's Gowns, and the Woman Who Makes Them', *Harper's Bazaar*, 9 January 1897.
81 Cunningham, 103.
82 Ribeiro, 46.
83 'Ellen Terry's "Portia" Costumes', *Aberdeen Journal*, 15 April 1880.
84 'Mr. Irving's Macbeth', *New York Times*, 30 December 1888.
85 *Manchester Weekly Times*, 12 January 1889.
86 *Era*, 19 January 1885.
87 *Manchester Weekly Times*, 12 January 1889.
88 'The Ladies' Column', *Leicester Chronicle*, 28 February 1880.
89 'Shop-Window Celebrity', *Belfast Newsletter*, 14 December 1885.

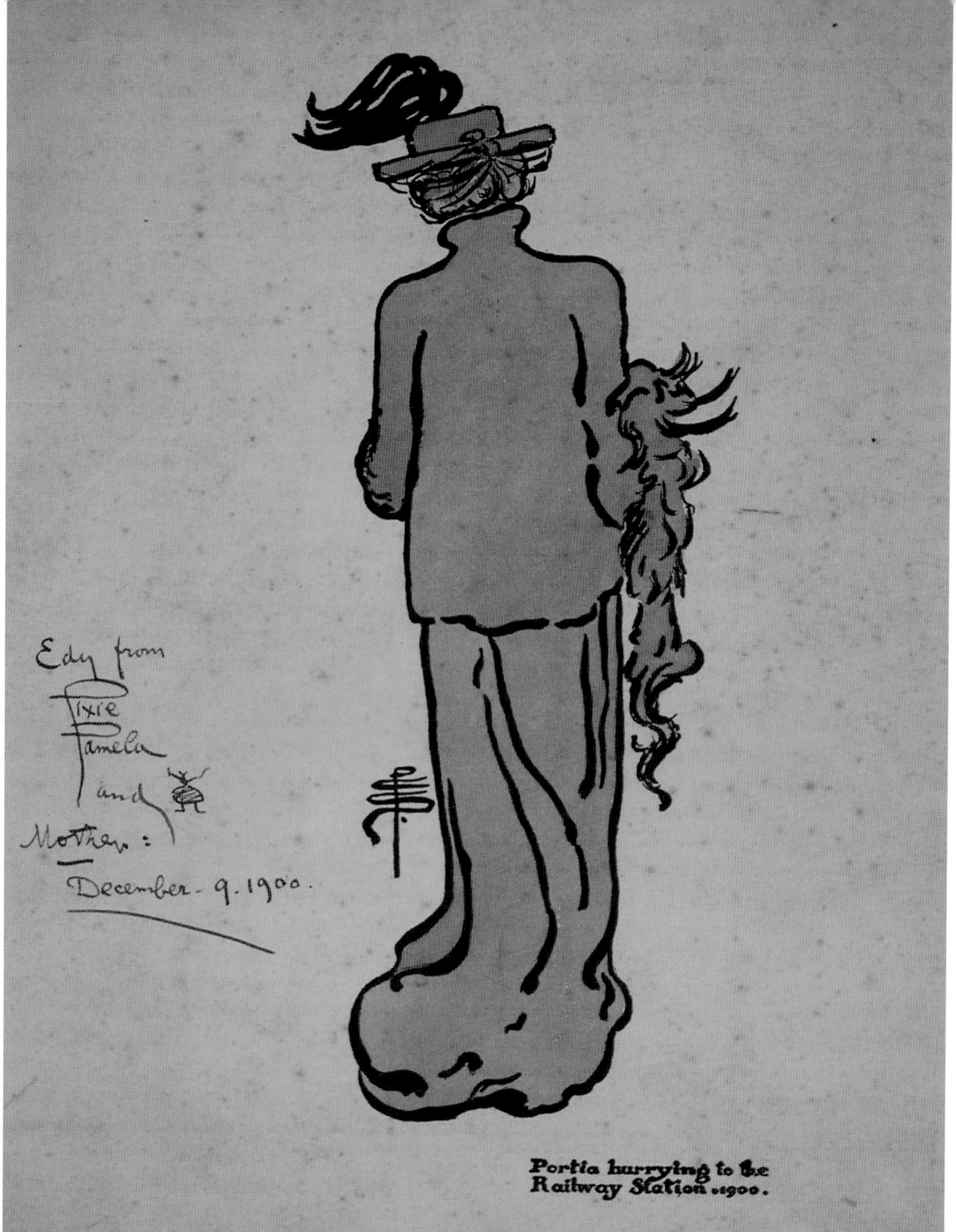
Edy from
Pixie
Pamela
and
Mother:
December-9.1900.
Portia hurrying to the
Railway Station .1900.

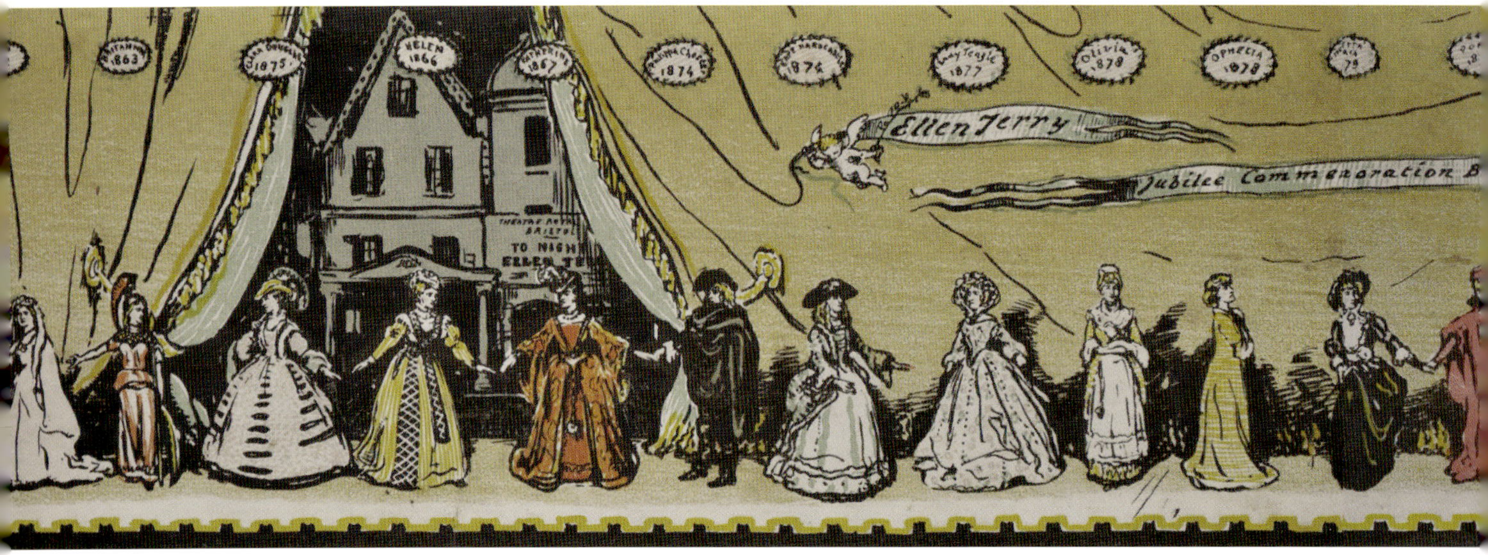
HELEN
1866
1874
1877
Olivia
1878
OPHELIA
1878
Ellen Terry
TO NIGHT